Eighth International Joint Conference on Natural Language Processing (IJCNLP 2017)

System Demonstrations

Taipei, Taiwan
1 December 2017

ISBN: 978-1-5108-5294-5

IJCNLP 2017

The Eighth International Joint Conference on Natural Language Processing

Proceedings of the IJCNLP 2017, System Demonstrations

November 27 December 1, 2017
Taipei, Taiwan

Preface

Welcome to the companion volume of the proceedings of IJCNLP 2017. This companion volume contains the contributions for the 8th International Joint Conference on Natural Language Processing which takes place from 27th November to 1st December in Taipei, Taiwan.

The primary aim of the system demonstrations program is to provide a chance to offer presentations of early research prototypes as well as interesting mature systems in all areas of natural language processing. The system demonstration co-chairs and the members of the program committee received 26 submissions, which is record-high in the IJCNLP history. Among the submissions, 17 outstanding papers were selected for inclusion in the program after reviews by three members of the program committee. We would like to thank all the members of the program committee for their excellent job in reviewing the submissions and providing their support for the final decision. In addition, we owe great thanks to other organizing committee members of IJCNLP 2017 including conference chair, program co-chairs, and local co-chairs for giving us great support.

Demonstration Co-chairs
Seong-Bae Park (Kyungpook National University, Korea)
Thepchai Supnithi (NECTEC, Thailand)

November 27 – December 1, 2017
Taipei, Taiwan

Co-chairs:

Seong-Bae Park, Kyungpook National University, Korea
Thepchai Supnithi, NECTEC, Thailand

Program Committee:

Prachya Boonkwan, NECTEC, Thailand
Paisarn Charoenpornsawat, CMU, USA
Atsushi Fujita, NICT, Japan
Caren Han, University of Tasmania, Australia
Choochart Haruechaiyasak, NECTEC, Thailand
Nongnuch Ketui, Thammasat University, Thailand
Harksoo Kim, Kangwon National University, Korea
Yu-Seop Kim, Hallym University, Korea
Mamoru Komachi, Tokyo Metropolitan University, Japan
Alisa Kongthon, NECTEC, Thailand
Krit Kosawat, NECTEC, Thailand
Prasert Luekhong, Rajamangala University of Technology Lanna, Thailand
Luong Chi Mai, IOIT, Vietnam
Seung-Hoon Na, Chonbuk National University, Korea
Win Pa Pa, University of Computer Studies, Myanmar
Rachel Roxas, National University, Philippines
Jeong-Woo Son, ETRI, Korea
Hyun-Je Song, Naver, Korea
Tasanawan Soonklang, Silpakorn University, Thailand
Masao Utiyama, NICT, Japan

Table of Contents

MASSAlign: Alignment and Annotation of Comparable Documents
Gustavo Paetzold, Fernando Alva-Manchego and Lucia Specia 1

CADET: Computer Assisted Discovery Extraction and Translation
Benjamin Van Durme, Tom Lippincott, Kevin Duh, Deana Burchfield, Adam Poliak, Cash Costello, Tim Finin, Scott Miller, James Mayfield, Philipp Koehn, Craig Harman, Dawn Lawrie, Chandler May, Max Thomas, Annabelle Carrell, Julianne Chaloux, Tongfei Chen, Alex Comerford, Mark Dredze, Benjamin Glass, Shudong Hao, Patrick Martin, Pushpendre Rastogi, Rashmi Sankepally, Travis Wolfe, Ying-Ying Tran and Ted Zhang 5

WiseReporter: A Korean Report Generation System
Yunseok Noh, Su Jeong Choi, Seong-Bae Park and Se-Young Park 9

Encyclolink: A Cross-Encyclopedia,Cross-language Article-Linking System and Web-based Search Interface
Yu-Chun Wang, Ka Ming Wong, Chun-Kai Wu, Chao-Lin Pan and Richard Tzong-Han Tsai . . . 13

A Telecom-Domain Online Customer Service Assistant Based on Question Answering with Word Embedding and Intent Classification
Jui-Yang Wang, Min-Feng Kuo, Jen-Chieh Han, Chao-Chuang Shih, Chun-Hsun Chen, Po-Ching Lee and Richard Tzong-Han Tsai 17

TOTEMSS: Topic-based, Temporal Sentiment Summarisation for Twitter
Bo Wang, Maria Liakata, Adam Tsakalidis, Spiros Georgakopoulos Kolaitis, Symeon Papadopoulos, Lazaros Apostolidis, Arkaitz Zubiaga, Rob Procter and Yiannis Kompatsiaris 21

MUSST: A Multilingual Syntactic Simplification Tool
Carolina Scarton, Alessio Palmero Aprosio, Sara Tonelli, Tamara Martín Wanton and Lucia Specia 25

XMU Neural Machine Translation Online Service
Boli Wang, Zhixing Tan, Jinming Hu, Yidong Chen and Xiaodong Shi 29

Semantics-Enhanced Task-Oriented Dialogue Translation: A Case Study on Hotel Booking
Longyue Wang, Jinhua Du, Liangyou Li, Zhaopeng Tu, Andy Way and Qun Liu 33

NNVLP: A Neural Network-Based Vietnamese Language Processing Toolkit
Hoang Pham, Pham Xuan Khoai, Tuan Anh Nguyen and Phuong Le-Hong 37

ClassifierGuesser: A Context-based Classifier Prediction System for Chinese Language Learners
Nicole Peinelt, Maria Liakata and Shu-Kai Hsieh 41

Automatic Difficulty Assessment for Chinese Texts
John Lee, Meichun Liu, Chun Yin Lam, Tak On Lau, Bing Li and Keying Li 45

Verb Replacer: An English Verb Error Correction System
Yu-Hsuan Wu, Jhih-Jie Chen and Jason Chang 49

Learning Synchronous Grammar Patterns for Assisted Writing for Second Language Learners
Chi-En Wu, Jhih-Jie Chen, Jim Chang and Jason Chang 53

Guess What: A Question Answering Game via On-demand Knowledge Validation
Yu-Sheng Li, Chien-Hui Tseng, Chian-Yun Huang and Wei-Yun Ma.........................57

STCP: Simplified-Traditional Chinese Conversion and Proofreading
Jiarui Xu, Xuezhe Ma, Chen-Tse Tsai and Eduard Hovy....................................61

Deep Neural Network based system for solving Arithmetic Word problems
Purvanshi Mehta, Pruthwik Mishra, Vinayak Athavale, Manish Shrivastava and Dipti Sharma . . 65

Conference Program

Tuesday November 28, 2017 (15:30 – 17:30)

MASSAlign: Alignment and Annotation of Comparable Documents
Gustavo Paetzold, Fernando Alva-Manchego and Lucia Specia

CADET: Computer Assisted Discovery Extraction and Translation
Benjamin Van Durme, Tom Lippincott, Kevin Duh, Deana Burchfield, Adam Poliak, Cash Costello, Tim Finin, Scott Miller, James Mayfield, Philipp Koehn, Craig Harman, Dawn Lawrie, Chandler May, Max Thomas, Annabelle Carrell, Julianne Chaloux, Tongfei Chen, Alex Comerford, Mark Dredze, Benjamin Glass, Shudong Hao, Patrick Martin, Pushpendre Rastogi, Rashmi Sankepally, Travis Wolfe, Ying-Ying Tran and Ted Zhang

WiseReporter: A Korean Report Generation System
Yunseok Noh, Su Jeong Choi, Seong-Bae Park and Se-Young Park

Encyclolink: A Cross-Encyclopedia,Cross-language Article-Linking System and Web-based Search Interface
Yu-Chun Wang, Ka Ming Wong, Chun-Kai Wu, Chao-Lin Pan and Richard Tzong-Han Tsai

A Telecom-Domain Online Customer Service Assistant Based on Question Answering with Word Embedding and Intent Classification
Jui-Yang Wang, Min-Feng Kuo, Jen-Chieh Han, Chao-Chuang Shih, Chun-Hsun Chen, Po-Ching Lee and Richard Tzong-Han Tsai

TOTEMSS: Topic-based, Temporal Sentiment Summarisation for Twitter
Bo Wang, Maria Liakata, Adam Tsakalidis, Spiros Georgakopoulos Kolaitis, Symeon Papadopoulos, Lazaros Apostolidis, Arkaitz Zubiaga, Rob Procter and Yiannis Kompatsiaris

MUSST: A Multilingual Syntactic Simplification Tool
Carolina Scarton, Alessio Palmero Aprosio, Sara Tonelli, Tamara Martín Wanton and Lucia Specia

XMU Neural Machine Translation Online Service
Boli Wang, Zhixing Tan, Jinming Hu, Yidong Chen and Xiaodong Shi

Semantics-Enhanced Task-Oriented Dialogue Translation: A Case Study on Hotel Booking
Longyue Wang, Jinhua Du, Liangyou Li, Zhaopeng Tu, Andy Way and Qun Liu

NNVLP: A Neural Network-Based Vietnamese Language Processing Toolkit
Hoang Pham, Pham Xuan Khoai, Tuan Anh Nguyen and Phuong Le-Hong

ClassifierGuesser: A Context-based Classifier Prediction System for Chinese Language Learners
Nicole Peinelt, Maria Liakata and Shu-Kai Hsieh

Automatic Difficulty Assessment for Chinese Texts
John Lee, Meichun Liu, Chun Yin Lam, Tak On Lau, Bing Li and Keying Li

Verb Replacer: An English Verb Error Correction System
Yu-Hsuan Wu, Jhih-Jie Chen and Jason Chang

Learning Synchronous Grammar Patterns for Assisted Writing for Second Language Learners
Chi-En Wu, Jhih-Jie Chen, Jim Chang and Jason Chang

Guess What: A Question Answering Game via On-demand Knowledge Validation
Yu-Sheng Li, Chien-Hui Tseng, Chian-Yun Huang and Wei-Yun Ma

STCP: Simplified-Traditional Chinese Conversion and Proofreading
Jiarui Xu, Xuezhe Ma, Chen-Tse Tsai and Eduard Hovy

Deep Neural Network based system for solving Arithmetic Word problems
Purvanshi Mehta, Pruthwik Mishra, Vinayak Athavale, Manish Shrivastava and Dipti Sharma

MASSAlign: Alignment and Annotation of Comparable Documents

Gustavo H. Paetzold and **Fernando Alva-Manchego** and **Lucia Specia**
Department of Computer Science
University of Sheffield, UK
{g.h.paetzold,f.alva,l.specia}@sheffield.ac.uk

Abstract

We introduce MASSAlign: a Python library for the alignment and annotation of monolingual comparable documents. MASSAlign offers easy-to-use access to state of the art algorithms for paragraph and sentence-level alignment, as well as novel algorithms for word-level annotation of transformation operations between aligned sentences. In addition, MASSAlign provides a visualization module to display and analyze the alignments and annotations performed.

1 Introduction

The ever-growing amount of information produced and distributed electronically has introduced a new challenge: adapting such information for different audiences. One may want, for example, to make their content available for speakers of as many languages as possible, or to make it more accessible for those with reading difficulties, such as those suffering from dyslexia and aphasia, or who are not native speakers of the language.

With that in mind, certain government institutions and content providers produce multiple versions of documents. The result are thousands of pairs of comparable articles, stories and other types of content that render the same information in different ways. Some examples are the European Parliament proceedings[1], which contains translated versions of speeches and other official communications, the Simple English Wikipedia[2], which offers simplified versions of Wikipedia articles; and the Newsela corpus (Xu et al., 2015), which provides versions of news articles for readers with various education levels.

[1]www.europarl.europa.eu
[2]http://simple.wikipedia.org

This data is very useful in the context of Natural Language Processing (NLP): it can be used in the training of automatic translators, simplifiers and summarizers that automate the process of adapting content. In order to do so, machine learning algorithms benefit from texts aligned at lower levels, such as paragraph, sentence, or even word levels. These alignments are however challenging to obtain since documents often do not even have the same number of sentences, i.e. they are *comparable* but not *parallel*. For monolingual texts, which are the focus of this paper, previous work has proposed different ways for obtaining sentence alignments: Xu et al. (2015) extract alignments based on a similarity metric, while Barzilay and Elhadad (2003) employ a more complex data-driven model, and Paetzold and Specia (2016) employ a vicinity-driven search method. However, we were not able to find any available and easy-to-use tool that allows one to align comparable documents at different levels of granularity. To solve that problem, we introduce MASSAlign: a user friendly tool that allows one to align monolingual comparable documents at both paragraph and sentence level, annotate words in aligned sentences with transformation labels, and also visualize the output produced.

2 System Overview

MASSAlign is a Python 2 library. It offers four main functionalities, which we describe in what follows: alignment at paragraph and sentence levels, word-level annotation of transformation operations, and output visualization.

2.1 Paragraph and Sentence Alignment

The `alignment` module of MASSAlign finds equivalent paragraphs and sentences in comparable documents. This module receives as input a pair of documents split at paragraph level and produces as output a series of paragraph alignments,

The Companion Volume of the IJCNLP 2017 Proceedings: System Demonstrations, pages 1–4,
Taipei, Taiwan, November 27 – December 1, 2017. ©2017 AFNLP

as well as sentence alignments within the aligned paragraphs. These alignments can be used in the creation of paragraph and sentence-level parallel corpora, which in turn can be employed in the training of models using machine learning.

The alignment method used by MASSAlign is that of Paetzold and Specia (2016), which employs a vicinity-driven approach. The algorithm first creates a similarity matrix between the paragraphs/sentences of aligned documents/paragraphs, using a standard bag-of-words TF-IDF model. It then finds a starting point to begin the search for an alignment path. The starting point is the coordinate in the matrix that is closest to [0,0] and holds a similarity score larger than α, which represents the minimum acceptable similarity for an alignment. They use $\alpha = 0.2$ for their experiments. From the starting point, it iteratively searches for good alignments in a hierarchy of vicinities. In each iteration, the alignment first checks if there is at least one acceptable alignment in the first vicinity. If so, it adds the coordinate with the highest similarity within the vicinity to the path. If not, it does the same to a second vicinity, then a third, and so on. The algorithm ends when it either (i) reaches one of the edges of the matrix, or (ii) fails to find an acceptable alignment. In their experiments, they use three vicinities. Given a coordinate $[i,j]$, they define its first vicinity as $V_1 = \{[i,j+1],[i+1,j],[i+1,j+1]\}$, its second vicinity as $V_2 = \{[i+1,j+2],[i+2,j+1]\}$, and its third vicinity V_3 as all remaining $[x,y]$ where $x>i$ and $y>j$.

We choose this alignment method for various reasons. First, it is one of the few that employs a hierarchical alignment approach, i.e. it exploits information from higher-level alignments to support and improve the quality of lower-level alignments. Moreover, the method can be used in documents that are not organized as a set of paragraphs: one can simply take each comparable document as a large paragraph and then apply the sentence-level alignment algorithm. The method is also entirely unsupervised and one can easily customize the alignment process by changing the similarity metric, the threshold α, or the sets of vicinities considered. Finally, this method has already been shown effective in Paetzold and Specia (2017), where it is used in the extraction of complex-to-simple word pairs from comparable documents to build lexical simplification models.

2.2 Word-Level Annotation

Once paragraphs and sentences have been aligned, one can analyze the differences between the two versions. For example, one can see that a sentence from an original news article was simplified into two others. Furthermore, MASSAlign allows one to obtain insights with respect to which transformation operations were performed at phrase or word-level. Some examples of operations include deletions, where words and/or phrases are discarded; and lexical simplifications, where words and/or phrases are replaced with more familiar alternatives. MASSAlign's `annotation` module provides novel algorithms that automatically identify deletions, substitutions, re-orderings, and additions of words and phrases.

The `annotation` module requires a pair of aligned sentences, their constituency parse trees, and the word alignments between them. To obtain word alignments, many consolidated tools can be employed, such as Giza++ (Och and Ney, 2003), fast_align (Dyer et al., 2013), and the monolingual word aligner (Sultan et al., 2014). Our annotation algorithms only require that the word alignments be in 1-index *Pharaoh* format, which can be obtained from any of the previously mentioned tools.

Our module first annotates word-level substitutions, deletions and additions: if two words are aligned and are not an exact match, the word in the original sentence receives a REPLACE tag; if a word in the original sentence is not aligned, it is annotated as a DELETE; and if a word in the modified sentence is not aligned, it is annotated as an ADD. There may be some cases of substitutions where two synonymous are not aligned. In order to improve the REPLACE labeling, we employ a simple heuristic: for every word in the original sentence labeled as DELETE, we check if there is a word in the modified sentence that (1) is labeled as ADD, (2) has the same position in the sentence, and (3) has the same part-of-speech tag. If these criteria are met, then the word label is changed to REPLACE. We also consider REWRITE as a special case of REPLACE or ADD where the words involved are isolated (i.e. no other word with the same label is next to it) and belong to a list of non-content words that we collected after a manual inspection of sample sentences.

We then proceed to labeling re-orderings (MOVE) by determining if the relative index of a word (considering preceding or following DELETEs and ADDs) in the original sentence changes in the modified one. Words that are kept, replaced or rewritten may be subject to re-orderings, such that a token may have more than one label (e.g. REPLACE and MOVE). For that, we extend the set of operations by the compound operations REPLACE+MOVE (RM) and REWRITE+MOVE (RWM).

In order to capture operations that span across syntactic units, such as phrases (chunks) or clauses, we group continuous operation labels for entire syntactic units using IOB notation. The constituent parse trees of the aligned sentences are used for this purpose. If the majority[3] of words within a syntactic unit in the sentence have the same label, the whole unit receives an operation label (for example, DELETE CLAUSE (DC)). We use this algorithm to label clauses and chunks[4], but in the latter case we do not use a particular unit label, and only rely on the IOB notation for the operation labels. Figure 1a presents an example of a DELETE labeling in chunks, while Figure 1b shows the unit label DELETE CLAUSE.

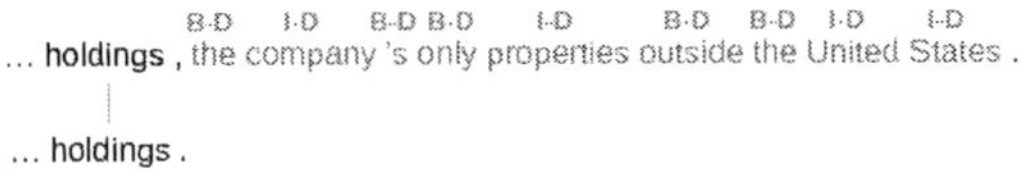

(a) Annotation of operations spanning chunks.

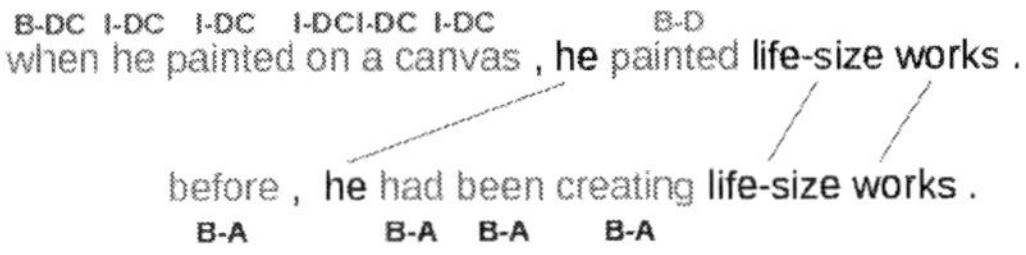

(b) Annotation of operations spanning a clause.

Figure 1: Examples of annotated sentence pairs where an operation label spans across a syntactic unit (chunk or clause).

For evaluation, we compared the algorithms' labels to manual annotations for 100 automatically aligned sentences of the Newsela corpus (Xu et al., 2015)[5]. This corpus consists of news articles and their simplifications, produced manually by professional editors. We achieved a micro-averaged F_1 score of 0.61. For 30 of those sentences, we calculated the pairwise inter-annotator agreement for 4 annotators, with average kappa = 0.57. The annotation algorithms are mainly effective at identifying additions, deletions and substitutions.

2.3 Visualization

The alignments and annotations produced by MASSAlign can be used not only for the creation of parallel corpora, but also for analysis purposes. One can, for example, inspect the sentence alignments between original and simplified documents to find which types of syntactic and semantic transformations with respect to content were made throughout the simplification process. To that purpose, MASSAlign provides a minimalistic graphical interface through its `visualization` module that exhibits paragraph and sentence alignments, as well as word-level annotations. Figures 2 and 3 illustrate these functionalities.

3 Demo Outline

Our demo will be combined with a poster which will show the functionalities of MASSAlign by illustrating how the tool can be used to create parallel corpora for text simplification. Participants will be able to test MASSAlign by producing and displaying alignments and annotations for different kinds of comparable documents on the fly.

4 Discussion and Future Work

We introduced MASSAlign: a Python 2 library that provides tools for the alignment, annotation and analysis of comparable monolingual documents. By using effective methods, MASSAlign is capable of aligning comparable documents at both paragraph and sentence level, annotating aligned sentences at word-level with fine-grained transformation labels, and displaying the alignments and annotations produced in an intuitive fashion.

Through these tools, MASSAlign can create parallel corpora from comparable documents and allow one to analyse the differences between them. MASSAlign was developed following simple software engineering principles such that it can be easily extended with new alignment, annotation and visualisation methods.

In the future, we aim to add to MASSAlign other supervised and unsupervised sentence-level alignment methods, such as the ones of Xu et al.

---

[3]We consider "majority" as at least 75%, to counteract the effect of incorrect labels caused by word misalignments.

[4]Our definition of "chunk" follows that of the CoNLL 2000 Shared Task: `http://www.cnts.ua.ac.be/conll2000/chunking`.

[5]The Newsela Article Corpus was downloaded from `https://newsela.com/data`, version 2016-01-29.

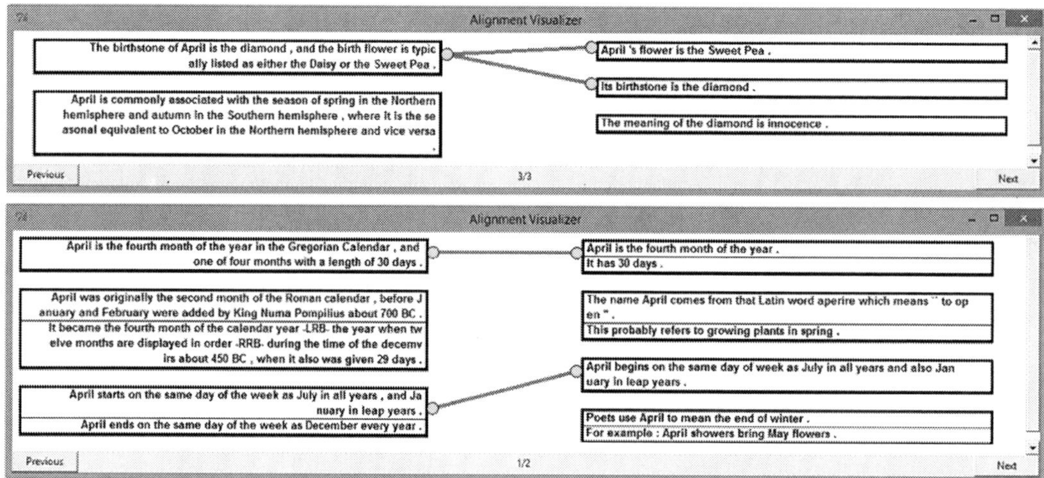

Figure 2: MASSAlign's visualisation interface for alignments.

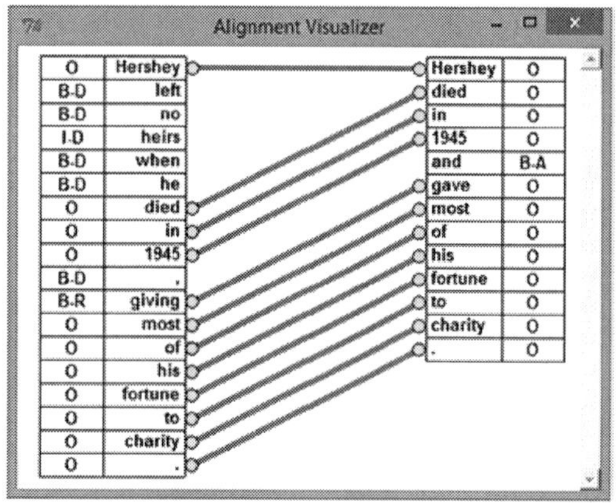

Figure 3: MASSAlign's visualisation interface for annotations.

(2015), Kajiwara and Komachi (2016), Bott and Saggion (2011), and Barzilay and Elhadad (2003), as well as built-in word alignment methods, such as the ones in (Dyer et al., 2013) and (Sultan et al., 2014). By doing so, the tool will become more self-contained and more flexible.

MASSAlign is available for download at `https://github.com/ghpaetzold/massalign` under a BSD license.

Acknowledgements

This work was partly supported by the EC project SIMPATICO (H2020-EURO-6-2015, grant number 692819).

References

Regina Barzilay and Noemie Elhadad. 2003. Sentence alignment for monolingual comparable corpora. In *Proceedings of EMNLP*, pages 25–32.

Stefan Bott and Horacio Saggion. 2011. An unsupervised alignment algorithm for text simplification corpus construction. In *Proceedings of the 2011 MTTG*, pages 20–26.

Chris Dyer, Victor Chahuneau, and Noah Smith. 2013. A simple, fast, and effective reparameterization of IBM model 2. In *Proceedings of NAACL*, pages 644–648.

Tomoyuki Kajiwara and Mamoru Komachi. 2016. Building a monolingual parallel corpus for text simplification using sentence similarity based on alignment between word embeddings. In *Proceedings of COLING*, pages 1147–1158.

Franz Josef Och and Hermann Ney. 2003. A systematic comparison of various statistical alignment models. *Computational Linguistics*, 29(1):19–51.

Gustavo H. Paetzold and Lucia Specia. 2017. Lexical simplification with neural ranking. In *Proceedings of EACL*, pages 34–40.

Gustavo Henrique Paetzold and Lucia Specia. 2016. Vicinity-driven paragraph and sentence alignment for comparable corpora. *arXiv preprint arXiv:1612.04113*.

Md Sultan, Steven Bethard, and Tamara Sumner. 2014. Back to basics for monolingual alignment: Exploiting word similarity and contextual evidence. *TACL*, 2:219–230.

Wei Xu, Chris Callison-Burch, and Courtney Napoles. 2015. Problems in current text simplification research: New data can help. *TACL*, 3:283–297.

CADET: Computer Assisted Discovery Extraction and Translation

**Benjamin Van Durme, Tom Lippincott, Kevin Duh, Deana Burchfield,
Adam Poliak, Cash Costello, Tim Finin, Scott Miller, James Mayfield
Philipp Koehn, Craig Harman, Dawn Lawrie, Chandler May, Max Thomas
Annabelle Carrell, Julianne Chaloux, Tongfei Chen, Alex Comerford
Mark Dredze, Benjamin Glass, Shudong Hao, Patrick Martin, Pushpendre Rastogi
Rashmi Sankepally, Travis Wolfe, Ying-Ying Tran, Ted Zhang**
Human Language Technology Center of Excellence, Johns Hopkins University

Abstract

Computer Assisted Discovery Extraction
and Translation (CADET) is a workbench
for helping knowledge workers find, label, and translate documents of interest. It
combines a multitude of analytics together
with a flexible environment for customiz-
ing the workflow for different users. This
open-source framework allows for easy
development of new research prototypes
using a micro-service architecture based
atop Docker and Apache Thrift.[1]

1 Introduction

CADET is an integrated workbench for helping
knowledge workers discover, extract, and translate
useful information. The user interface (Figure 1)
is based on a domain expert starting with a large
collection of data, wishing to *discover* the subset
that is most salient to their goals, and exporting
the results to tools for either *extraction* of specific
information of interest or interactive *translation*.

For example, imagine a humanitarian aid
worker with a large collection of social media
messages obtained in the aftermath of a natural
disaster. Her goal is to find messages that contain
specific needs, such as hospitals requiring food or
medical supplies. She may begin by performing
a textual search in our *Discovery* interface (Figure 2). The *Discovery* interface can be customized
with different types of search providers, and the
aid worker can provide relevance feedback to per-
sonalize her search results. After several search
sessions, the aid worker may wish to automatically
construct a spreadsheet that contains the relevant

---

[1]Please see `http://hltcoe.github.io/cadet`
for more information. The demo consists of a running system (both online and locally on a laptop), as well as pointers
for building the software.

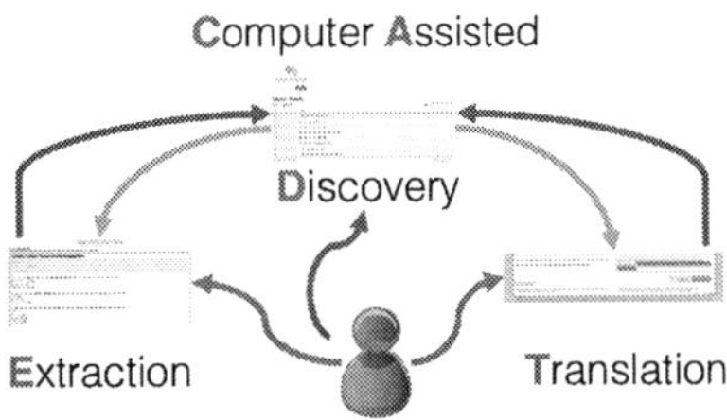

Figure 1: CADET concept

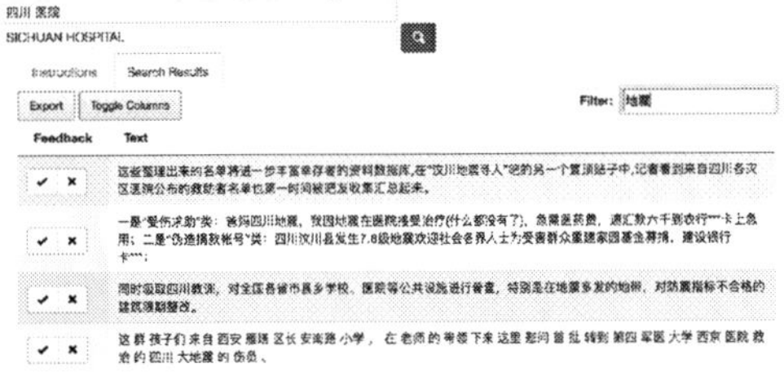

Figure 2: Discovery user interface

information in structured form. To do so, she exports the search results to our *Extraction* interface,
where she can provide annotations to help train an
information extraction system. The *Extraction* interface allows the user to label any text span using
any schema, and also incorporates active learning
to complement the discovery process in selecting
data to annotate.

Now consider a different user of the same data:
suppose a citizen reporter wishes to provide up-
to-date news to foreign audiences. He uses our
Discovery interface to find the messages needed
for his story, then exports the text to our *Translation* interface. The *Translation* interface is a
computer-assisted translation toolkit that enables
him to quickly translate the messages to the target
foreign language.

The challenge with building these personalized
workflows is that it involves integration of dis-
parate technologies and software components. Individual components like search, information extraction, active learning, and machine translation

5

may already be open-sourced and extensible, but to make all these components talk to each other requires a non-trivial amount of effort. CADET is a prototyping framework that demonstrates how this integration can be made easier using a micro-service architecture built on Docker and Thrift.[2]

2 Architecture Design

Data serialization In order for analytics to be easily integrated, we developed CONCRETE[3], a data serialization format for Human Language Technology (HLT). It replaces ad-hoc XML, CSV, or programming language-specific serialization as a way of storing document- and sentence- level annotations. CONCRETE is based on Apache Thrift and thus works cross-platform and in almost all popular programming languages, including Javascript, C++, Java, and Python. All analytics in CADET, such as search providers or information extraction systems, are required to be "concrete compliant".

Microservices Analytics within CADET are implemented using a microservice architecture and served up as Docker containers[4]. This allows for rapid prototyping without worrying about the various underlying programming languages and library dependencies. The containers talk via a common CONCRETE microservice API. CADET consists of a set of these microservices that provide functionality for fetching and storing documents, searching, annotating, and training. These service definitions then support code generation of clients and servers in a wide range of languages including Python, Java, C++, Perl, and JavaScript. The decoupled microservice design combined with Thrift's code generation allows researchers to rapidly integrate their own HLT components or compose workflows from existing components.

Platforms CADET workflows have been run in a variety of environments: from standalone laptops with no connection to the internet, to the grid environment, to demonstration systems hosted on Amazon Web Services. Data storage is abstracted, with implementations supporting a simple file-backed directory structure, up to a network distributed Apache Accumulo instance. Each component is a Docker container which can be downloaded, run, and mixed-and-matched based on the need. This framework was used as the basis of a popular course at JHU, with undergraduate students cloning entire frameworks, developing both on laptops and on AWS for projects on knowledge discovery in text.[5]

3 Discovery

Discovery in CADET is presented to the user as a basic IR interface (Figure 2): a query is entered, results are returned in snippet format in a ranked list. These may be additionally labeled for relevance-feedback, interacted with for visualizing pre-computed HLT annotations stored with CONCRETE, or exported to either translation or extraction services. A major goal in the design of the discovery micro-services was to allow for abstracting a large number of non-traditional IR mechanisms, through a common and simple interface. The CADET admin interface allows for on-the-fly changing out of different discovery service providers, in order to allow for compare and contrast studies in how well one perspective on search may be more beneficial than another to a given user. Current discovery providers include:

Keyword search Our baseline discovery approach is keyword search supported by a module implementing our microservice APIs and using the Lucene information retrieval library.[6] This analytic is aware of the Concrete COMMUNICATION data structure, taking a collection of processed communications and performing standard bag of word indexing using the existing document tokenizations.

Cross-lingual For demonstrating the ease of extending the existing pipelines we have implemented an English-Chinese transliteration engine, which is beneficial in particular to named entity search. Many names are transliterated, i.e. characters of Chinese entities may be spelled out in terms of the Latin alphabet, where for an English-speaking user it may be easier to issue queries using the English transliteration, rather than the

---

[2]CADET is the result of a 9-week summer workshop at the Johns Hopkins University Human Language Technology Center of Excellence (JHU HLTCOE). A motivation for the workshop was the observation that: *there are many more potential users of HLT, each with their own needs, than there are researchers to customize technology to those needs.* Our goal with CADET, besides the workbench itself, is to demonstrate an approach for rapid prototyping and integration.

[3]http://hltcoe.github.io/concrete

[4] https://www.docker.com

[5]This course has recently won an internal educational award at JHU (Lippincott & Van Durme).

[6]https://lucene.apache.org

original Chinese. We currently support a query transliteration system based on an approach similar to Finch and Sumita (2008).

Question Answering From keywords to natural language sentences, one of the CADET discovery service providers is a fully integrated version of recent JHU work in discriminative IR for question answer passage retrieval (Chen and Van Durme, 2017). This allows users to type in a query and get back individual sentences ranked by their likelihood of answering the question.

Mention search We define *entity mention search* as the task of selecting a mention (name, nominal or pronominal) in a currently viewed document, and returning documents most likely to contain mentions of the same entity. We implemented mention search wrapped on top of KELVIN (Finin et al., 2016) which is a multi-year investment in knowledge base population (KBP) research. This framework processes a provided document collection ahead of time to create a knowledge graph with information about entities and their properties, relations and mentions. Mention queries on a pre-processed document interpreted by the KELVIN search service provider as a lookup against a constructed KB, with the provenance information – mentions across the corpus supporting a given entity – returned for displaying to the user. This is an example of ongoing work at the HLTCOE in recasting KBP as supporting technology for structured information retrieval.

Entity Search We define *entity search* as the task of selecting entities from a KB that are similar to a set of entities queried. We implemented Bayesian Sets algorithm and a neural variational auto-encoder version (in preparation), and a user can switch between them using the admin interface. We also provide "query rationale" to explain why a particular entity was returned by displaying important token features for the entities as well as important mentions associated to each entity.

Topic Search We support discovery through notion of "topic search", where documents are analyzed with a topic model and are ranked according to a minimization of Jensen-Shannon divergence between the document's topic distribution and the inferred topic representation of the keywords of a query. Our topic model (JHU Brightside) is a C library implementing stochastic variational inference (Hoffman et al., 2013) for the latent Dirichlet allocation (LDA) (Blei et al., 2003) among others.

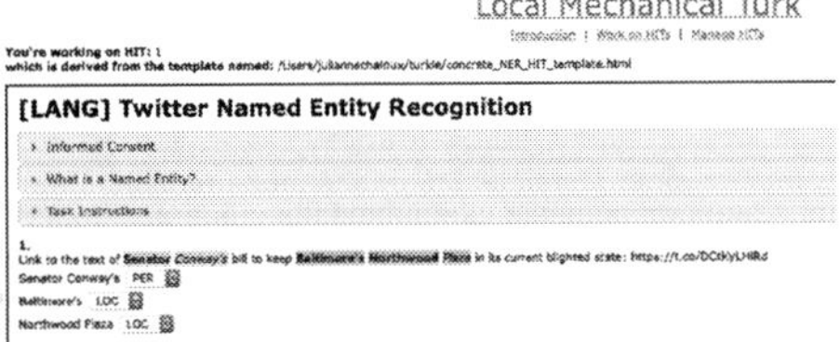

Figure 3: Extraction annotation interface

4 Extraction

After selecting content via the Discovery services, the user can switch to the Extraction web interface to build an information extraction system. CADET provides an interface (Figure 3) for the user to efficiently label this data according to their own sequence tagging schemas, e.g., for named entity recognition (NER).

The extraction annotation framework is also built on CONCRETE, supporting the application of multiple competing systems on content, storing those results together in a single data object, and then visualizing the results back to the user for potential correction. User feedback is stored alongside automatic system results, with annotations from an arbitrary number of users able to stored and easily retrieved later. A user may either correct existing system annotations for later retraining, or existing annotations may be used purely in an active learning service.

Active Learning As CADET is oriented around personalization for a knowledge worker, active learning (AL) is a core consideration, abstracted through a handful of microservice definitions. Interactions between an extraction annotation front-end and learning in the back-end is handled asynchronously by a *data broker*. Content by default is presented to a user for annotation in the rank order provided by a given discovery service, but as a user provides annotations a model may be actively (re-)trained in the background, communicating a preference for new annotations back to the broker, which will reorder subsequent units provided to one or more clients.

Like other services in the CONCRETE stack, the AL service, refered to as LEARN[7], is a specification that can be implemented in any programming language supported by Thrift. The LEARN micro-service's flexibility allows a developer to determine how often the AL server returns a sorted list to the client: a given model implementation

---

[7]http://hltcoe.github.io/concrete/schema/learn.html

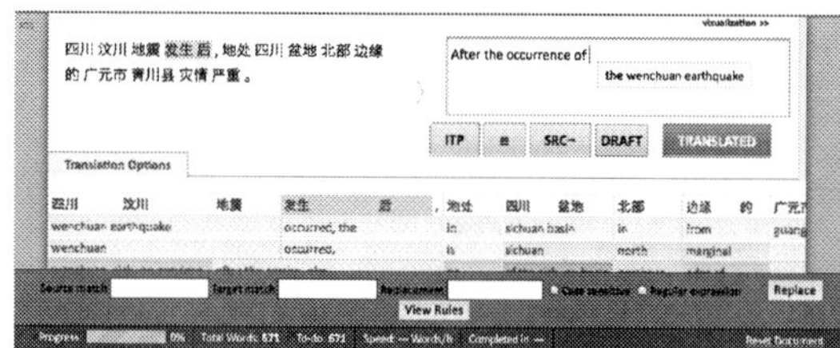

Figure 4: Translation User interface (CASMACAT). The user can see the source sentence (e.g. in Chinese) on the left pane, and can type in or post-edit the translation (e.g. in English) on the right pane.

may be slow to retrain when provided new annotations (such as if retraining in batch mode, from scratch), or be quick to update (such as if supporting incremental training). As the broker moderates the client interaction, then no matter the promptness of the AL backend, the annotator(s) will always have work to do, determined by the most recent update to the annotation ordering.

Information Extraction (IE) systems We have implemented two IE systems under CADET. (1) Pacaya[8] is a Java-based graphical model toolkit (Gormley, 2015) with models that supports tasks such as NER and semantic role labeling. (2) Milner is a sequence-tagging model based on a Hidden Markov Model with Discriminatively Trained Observation Probabilities. This resembles SVM-HMMs, but uses a logistic regression model in place of an SVM for the output. This system was designed foremost for fast training and application on new data.

5 Translation

CADET allows users to export foreign-language documents collected in the discovery phase for translation into e.g. English. We employ CASMACAT (Alabau et al., 2014)[9] (Figure 4) which provides capabilities for: (1) *Post-editing*: first the source sentence is automatically translated by a machine translation system such as Moses (Koehn et al., 2007), followed by a user editing any part of the translated text in order to improve the translation quality; and (2) *Interactive translation prediction*: similar to the auto-complete feature of text input on mobile devices, interactive translation prediction improves translation speed by reducing the number of keystrokes needed in typing. This interface enables the user to create bitext on

[8] https://github.com/mgormley/pacaya-nlp
[9] http://www.casmacat.eu

the discovered documents and improve machine translation in the domain of interest.

6 Conclusion

CADET is a framework for rapidly prototyping HLT workflows around a user's needs. We demonstrated a system that enables the knowledge worker to discover material, then actively annotate training data for information extraction or machine translation systems. The underlying principles of our microservice design architecture, based on Docker and Thrift, allows for the combination of a wide variety of analytics. We have built a number of modules that support different microservice definitions such as discovery and active learning, and new developments with different user workflows are planned for the future.

References

Vicent Alabau, Christian Buck, Michael Carl, Francisco Casacuberta, Mercedes García-Martínez, Ulrich Germann, Jesús González-Rubio, Robin Hill, Philipp Koehn, Luis Leiva, Bartolomé Mesa-Lao, Daniel Ortiz-Martínez, Herve Saint-Amand, Germán Sanchis Trilles, and Chara Tsoukala. 2014. Casmacat: A computer-assisted translation workbench. In *EACL*.

David M. Blei, Andrew Y. Ng, and Michael I. Jordan. 2003. Latent Dirichlet allocation. *JMLR*.

Tongfei Chen and Benjamin Van Durme. 2017. Discriminative Information Retrieval for Question Answering Sentence Selection. In *EACL*.

Andrew Finch and Eiichiro Sumita. 2008. Phrase-based machine transliteration. In *TCAST*.

Tim Finin, Dawn Lawrie, James Mayfield, Paul McNamee, Jessa Laspesa, and Micheal Latman. 2016. HLTCOE participation in TAC KBP 2016: Cold start and EDL. In *Ninth Text Analysis Conference*.

Matthew R. Gormley. 2015. *Graphical Models with Structured Factors, Neural Factors, and Approximation-Aware Training*. Ph.D. thesis, Johns Hopkins University, Baltimore, MD.

Matthew D. Hoffman, David M. Blei, Chong Wang, and John Paisley. 2013. Stochastic variational inference. *JMLR*.

Philipp Koehn, Hieu Hoang, Alexandra Birch, Chris Callison-Burch, Marcello Federico, Nicola Bertoldi, Brooke Cowan, Wade Shen, Christine Moran, Richard Zens, Chris Dyer, Ondrej Bojar, Alexandra Constantin, and Evan Herbst. 2007. Moses: Open source toolkit for statistical machine translation. In *ACL*.

WiseReporter: A Korean Report Generation System

Yunseok Noh and **Su Jeong Choi** and **Seong-Bae Park** and **Se-Young Park**
School of Computer Science and Engineering
Kyungpook National University
Daegu, Korea
{ysnoh,sjchoi,sbpark}@sejong.knu.ac.kr   seyoung@knu.ac.kr

Abstract

We demonstrate a report generation system called *WiseReporter*. The WiseReporter generates a text report of a specific topic which is usually given as a keyword by verbalizing knowledge base facts involving the topic. This demonstration does not demonstate only the report itself, but also the processes how the sentences for the report are generated. We are planning to enhance WiseReporter in the future by adding data analysis based on deep learning architecture and text summarization.

1 Introduction

The necessity of well-organized information about emerging topics grows fast, but the conventional search engines such as Google or Bing provide just a list of relevant documents. Since the results of the search engines are unstructured, there should be additional and expensive cost to provide users with exact information. However, due to extremely large volume of information amount, it is nearly impossible for users themselves to look over all contents and get the insight of topics of interest from them. From this point of view, we argue the need of a tool which enables analyzing a large volume of documents and summarizing them as a report that can be easily understood by the users.

As the very first step of the report generation tool, we demonstrate a prototype system called *WiseReporter* that translates knowledges in a knowledge base (KB) to text reports. There exist many large scale KBs such as Freebase and DBpedia, and several algorithms to add knowledges from web documents into a KB automatially (Carlson et al., 2010). Therefore, in this demonstration of WiseReporter, we focus only on the verbalization of the facts in a KB to generate a report for a specific topic.

Basically, WiseReporter is a template based generation system (Mellish et al., 2006). This approach has been broadly used for generating natural language texts from KB facts (Nadjet et al., 2014), where a KB fact consists of a relation and two entities linked by the relation. If there are natural language templates for every relation in a KB, then the facts can be easily transformed into natural language sentences by filling slots of the proper template with the entities of the facts. In addition to the templates and template-slot-filling, WiseReporter contains many processes for report generation such as macro- and micro-planning, and surface-form realization.

In this demonstration, we use two KBs for text report generation. One is a manually-constructed domain-specific KB associated with IT products, and the other is DBpedia to cover more general topics. With the KBs, we prove that WiseReporter provides reasonable results in terms of *linguistic quality* evaluation of DUC task, and also demonstrate how sentences of a report are generated from the KBs by visualizing some generation rules.

2 Overview of WiseReporter

2.1 System Architecture

WiseReporter adopts a pipelined architecture for natural language generation following several studies on ontology verbalization (Androutsopoulos et al., 2013; Nadjet et al., 2014). The architecture is typically composed with three major modules (Mellish et al., 2006): (i) text planning (also referred to as macro-planning), (ii) sentence planning (also known as micro-planning), and (iii) surface-form realization. The text planning module is responsible for choosing *what to say* and organizing the selected content in a coherent way. The sentence planning module is re-

9

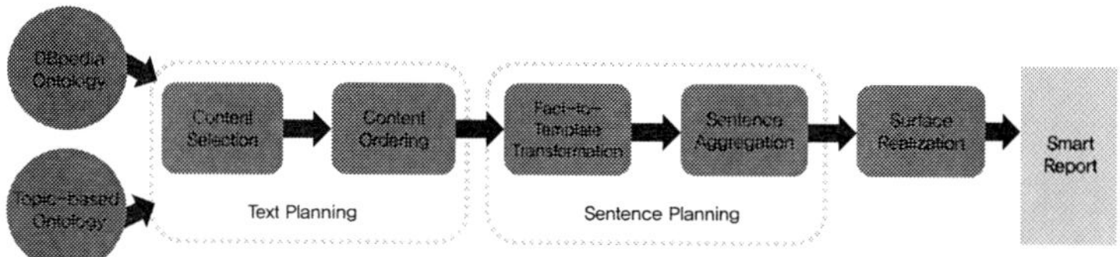

Figure 1: The overall pipelined architecture of WiseReporter.

sponsible for mapping the text plan to a linguistic structure, grouping information into sentences, and performing aggregation and lexicalization. At last, the surface-form realizer is in charge of rendering each sentence plan into a sentence string.

WiseReporter actually implements the pipelined architecture with the following five components (see Figure 1).

- **Content selection**. Both open planning and closed planning (Nadjet et al., 2014) are used for IT product KB and DBpedia respectively.

- **Content ordering**. Following the work of Androutsopoulos et al. (2013), we focus on enhancing local coherence by considering smooth topic change among adjacent sentences.

- **Fact-to-template transformation**. The rules for fact-to-template transformation are carefully designed with the consideration for Korean language phenomena such as Subject-Object-Verb (SOV) word-order and decision of postposition (*josa*) (Yang, 1995).

- **Sentence aggregation**. Several aggregation rules are applied to merging multiple simple sentences into a complex sentence. This step allows various and fluent natural language expressions.

- **Surface realization**. This component deals with several issues about realization of Korean surface-form including the problem of determining verbal endings (Yang, 1995). Especially, the endings related to tense, conjunction, and passive expressions are treated intensively.

The generated report consists of a number of paragraphs and an image related to the report topic. The image is inserted for helping users understand the generated texts better, and this image is simply obtained by Google image search. The typical layout of the report is pre-defined in this version of WiseReporter. The automatic layout arrangement and the appropriate image selection (or generation) remain as our future work.

We evaluated the quality of the generated reports by human judgement. The linguistic quality evaluation for summarization was taken from the previous study of Over et al. (2007). Five native evaluators were asked to score the generated reports from 1 to 5 points on five evaluation items of grammaticality, non-redundancy, structure and coherence, referential clarity, and focus (Over et al., 2007). The grand average score on 10 reports was 3.6 of 5.0. This result is competitive with the average score of 1.96 at the work of Androutsopoulos et al. (2013)[1].

2.2 Knowledge Bases

WiseReporter makes use of two KBs for report generation. One is a domain-specific ontology constructed manually, and the other is DBpedia. Domain-specific ontologies are usually designed to represent specifications of a subject, but this is not enough for report generation to deliver information such as background or related events. Therefore, an ontology is designed that describes IT products in detail by analyzing the documents on IT products. For this, a number of natural language patterns are collected, and then many facts are harvested from the documents by pattern matching the patterns with the documents (Gerber and Ngomo, 2012). After that, the collected facts are refined manually for accuracy. The final IT product KB contains 239 facts in total.

In addition to domain-specific ontology in hand, DBpedia is also included in WiseReporter for wide coverage of the system. In order to generate reports for the topics in DBpedia, we defined 167 templates. After all, WiseReporter can produce reports on 29,255 different topics.

---

[1]This study evaluted their system by 1 to 3 scale on English texts from Wine Ontology.

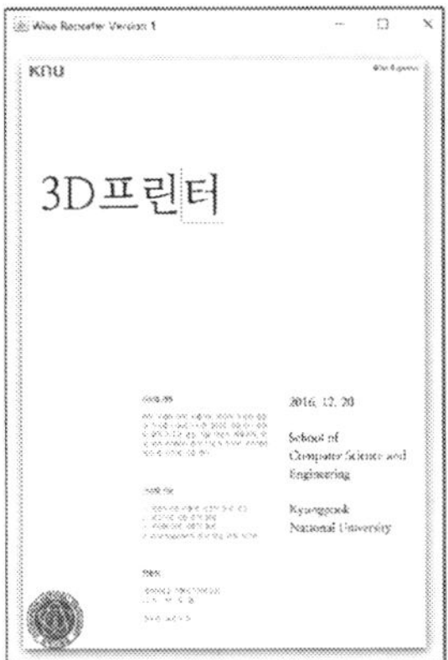

Figure 2: The report cover interface with the title
'3D 프린터 (3D printer)' inputed by a user.

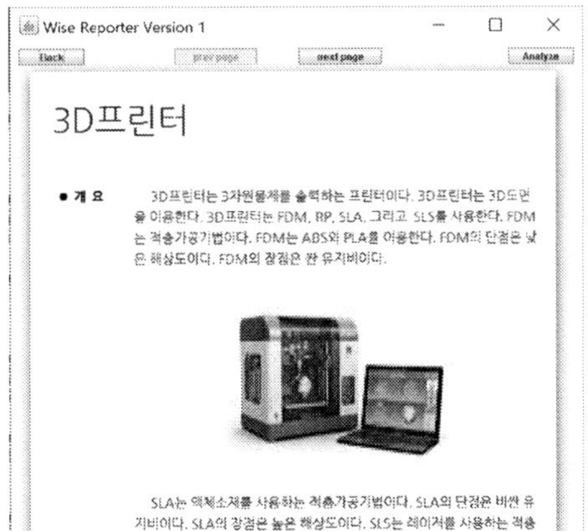

Figure 3: The report about '3D printer' generated
by WiseReporter. This result is generated by using
our IT product KB.

3 Outline of Demonstration

The following three steps outline our demonstration:

1. WiseReporter accepts a keyword such as '3D
   프린터 (3D printer)' in the title position of
   the report cover interface (see Figure 2).

2. WiseReporter returns a text report including an image about the topic if our domain-
   specifc KB or DBpedia has facts related to
   the keyword (see Figure 3).

3. One can choose the *Analyze* button for
   switching the mode to demonstrate how each
   sentence in the report is generated (see Figure 4). In this mode, the system shows a list
   of KB facts and sentence generation rules that
   are actually used in generating each sentence.

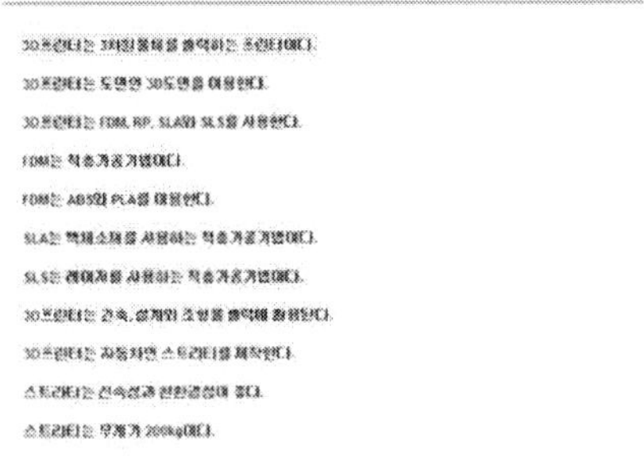

Figure 4: The interface of demonstration mode.
Each sentence is selectable for showing all information to generate the sentence.

3.1 Report Presentation

WiseReporter starts with the report cover interface as shown in Figure 2. This interface accepts
a keyword as the title of a report. That is, WiseReporter generates a report about the given keyword. The sample report in Figure 3 is about '3D
printer'. This report consists of two pages with a
number of paragraphs. It provides various information about '3D printer' including its definition,
resources, various mechanisms, and its pros and
cons.

3.2 Demonstration of Sentence Generation

Figure 4 shows the demonstration mode that is ac-
tivated by choosing the *Analyze* button located on
top right of the main report page. This mode lists
the sentences that appear in the report line by line.
Each sentence line can be selectable to demonstrate how the sentence is generated. The information provided is (i) the KB facts involved in the
sentence, (ii) the templates for the facts, and (iii)
the aggregation rules of the templates.

The system also shows the used KB facts as a
graph (see Figure 5). The facts involved in generating the selected sentence are easily recognized
as a red-colored part of the graph. The corresponding templates to the facts are also presented in Figure 5. These templates shows a notable SOV word-
order characteristic of Korean well.

Finally, we can see how WiseReporter forms
a complex sentence ("3D printer is a printer that
prints 3D objects.") from multiple single sentences
in Figure 6. The example of Figure 6 demonstrates
one of the rules combining two sentences which
share a common subject. The rule in this figure

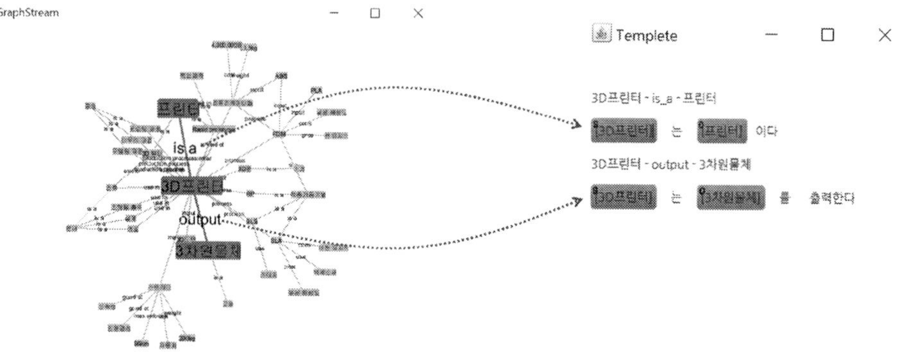

Figure 5: The graph presentation of the IT product KB focused on the topic of '3D printer' (left side). The nodes and edges marked with red color are the facts used to generate the first sentence "3D printer is a printer that prints 3D objects". The corresponding Korean templates to the facts are also presented on the right side.

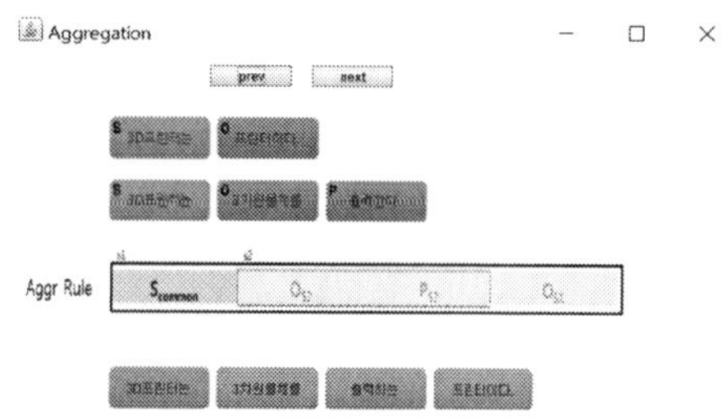

Figure 6: The demonstration screen capture of the sentence aggregation. Two templates are combined into a complex sentence template.

explains how a sentence ("3D printer is a printer.") embeds another sentence ("3D printer prints 3D objects.") when they share a subject.

4 Conclusion

In this paper, we briefly introduced WiseReporter, a prototype text report generation system, and our demonstration of the system at IJCNLP 2017. The system uses two KBs for getting information of topics of interest, and verbalizes the information coherently. We are planning to extend it in the future by going beyond KB verbalization. We also plan to make the system available to the public by transplanting the system as a web-based service.

Acknowledgments

This work was supported by Institute for Information & communications Technology Promotion(IITP) grant funded by the Korea government(MSIT) (No.2017-0-01772, Development of QA systems for Video Story Understanding to pass the Video Turing Test) and (No.2016-0-00145, Smart Summary Report Generation from Big Data Related to a Topic)

References

I. Androutsopoulos, G. Lampouras, and D. Galanis. 2013. Generating natural language descriptions from OWL ontologies: the naturalowl system. *Journal of Artificial Intelligence Research*, 48:671–715.

A. Carlson, J. Betteridge, B. Kisiel, B. Settles, E. Hruschka Jr, and T. Mitchell. 2010. Toward an architecture for Never-Ending Language Learning. In *Proceedings of the 24th AAAI Conference on Artificial Intelligence*, pages 1306–1313.

D. Gerber and A.-C. Ngomo. 2012. Extracting multilingual natural-language patterns for RDF predicates. In *Proceedings of the 18th International Conference on Knowledge Engineering and Knowledge Management*, pages 87–96.

C. Mellish, D. Scott, L. Cahill, D. Paiva, R. Evans, and M. Reape. 2006. A reference architecture for natural language generation systems. *Natural Language Engineering*, 12(1):1–34.

B.-A. Nadjet, G. Casamayor, and L. Wanner. 2014. Natural language generation in the context of the semantic web. *Semantic Web*, 5(6):493–513.

P. Over, H. Dang, and D. Harman. 2007. DUC in context. *Information Processing & Management*, 43(6):1506–1520.

W.-J. Yang. 1995. *Korean language generation in an interlingua-based speech translation system*. Ph.D. thesis, Massachusetts Institute of Technology.

Encyclolink: A Cross-Encyclopedia, Cross-language Article-Linking System and Web-based Search Interface

Yu-Chun Wang[1]   Ka Ming Wong[2]   Chun-Kai Wu[3]   Chao-Lin Pan[2]   Richard Tzong-Han Tsai[2*]

[1]Department of Buddhist Studies, Dharma Drum Institute of Liberal Arts, Taiwan

[2]Department of Computer Sciecne and Information Engineering, National Central University, Taiwan

[3]Department of Computer Sciecne, National Tsin Hua University, Taiwan

ycwang@dila.edu.tw   marketforwkm@gmail.com

j3rmp4d93@gmail.com   adhesivee@gmail.com   thtsai@ncu.edu.tw

Abstract

Cross-language article linking (CLAL) is the task of finding corresponding article pairs across encyclopedias of different languages. In this paper, we present Encyclolink, a web-based CLAL search interface designed to help users find equivalent encyclopedia articles in Baidu Baike for a given English Wikipedia article title query. Encyclolink is powered by our cross-encyclopedia entity embedding CLAL system (0.8 MRR). The browser-based interface provides users with a clear and easily readable preview of the contents of retrieved articles for comparison.

1 Introduction

Online encyclopedias are among the most frequently used Internet services today, providing information summaries on millions of topics in all branches of knowledge. Wikipedia is one of the largest online encyclopedias and has many language versions, but there are alternatives to Wikipedia in some languages. In China, for example, Baidu Baike and Hudong are the largest encyclopedia sites. However, since the various encyclopedias in different languages have no connections to each other, it makes it difficult for searchers to find comprehensive results drawn from multiple online encyclopedias in multiple languages. If all or some of the world's online encyclopedias were integrated in a "meta-encyclopedia", potentially even translated into a user's local language, it would greatly richen search and information retrieval, helping users explore multiple viewpoints on a topic from users of other languages.

---

*corresponding author

In this paper, we introduce Encyclolink, a system that links articles written in two different languages from two different encyclopedia platforms, allowing users to search and browse information from two online encyclopedias in one interface. Encyclolink is based on cross-language article linking (CLAL), the task of creating links between equivalent articles written in different languages from different encyclopedias. Using Encyclolink, a user can input an English query and then see all linked Chinese articles in order of relevance. The user can then browse the English article and its Chinese counterpart side by side for comparison.

2 Related Work

Cross-language article linking is a new research target. The related work can be mainly divided into two groups: CLAL on Wikipedia and CLAL on different encyclopedias.

2.1 CLAL across Wikipedia Language Versions

The first work that aimed to find new cross-language links between English and German is Sorg and Cimiano (2008). They proposed a chain link hypothesis, which assumes that for any two cross-lingual linked articles, there are chain links in many language versions between them. They designed a candidate selection process based on the hypothesis and built a classifier with text-based features to predict the links.

Oh et al. (2008) later designed a language-independent approach. They first converted every English and Japanese Wikipedia article into vectors of the link, text and context of that article. Then they translated English vectors into Japanese using a dictionary created from existing cross-language links. Finally they adopted BM-25 to compute similarity between these vectors to select candidate links.

13

The Companion Volume of the IJCNLP 2017 Proceedings: System Demonstrations, pages 13–16,
Taipei, Taiwan, November 27 – December 1, 2017. ©2017 AFNLP

Wang et al. (2012), on the other hand, relied solely on link structure between English and Chinese Wikipedia articles. They found out that the more common links or categories there are between two cross-lingual articles, the more likely they are to be equivalent articles. They first created a graph for each Wikipedia version; nodes in the graph represent articles and edges are hyperlinks between articles. Then, they used the cross-language links between two Wikipedia versions to reconnect two graphs in a pair-wise connectivity graph (PCG), which served as the structure of their learning model.

2.2 CLAL between Wikipedia and Baidu Baike

Wang et al. (2012) attempted to integrate two different encyclopedias, English Wikipedia and Chinese Baidu Baike, into one cross-language encyclopedia. They created over 0.2 million links between the encyclopedias, but their approach requires many manually pre-linked article links and category links to create the pair-wise connectivity graph (PCG) model. Furthermore, in the paper, they do not mention how to verify accuracy of the newly discovered cross-language links.

Another relevant work is Wang et al. (2014), which also focuses on linking English Wikipedia and Baidu Baike articles. To select and predict article links, they designed text-related features for an SVM classifier. Their features include bidirectional title matching, title similarity, hypernym translation and English title occurrence.

3 Methods

Given an article from a knowledge base (KB), CLAL aims to find the article's corresponding article in another KB of a different language. Corresponding articles are defined as articles describing the same entity in different languages. Following Wang et al.'s (2014) example, we also divide CLAL into two stages: candidate selection and candidate ranking. The candidates for each Wikipedia article are selected with the Lucene search engine, and the queries and documents are translated with the Google Translate API. We then train an SVM classifier with the same features described in Wang et al.'s (2014) paper. The given English Wikipedia article and a candidate Baidu article are denoted as w and b. Wang et al.'s (2014) features are as follows:

- BM25: w's title is translated into Chinese and then used as a query to retrieve articles from Baidu Baike with the Lucene search engine. The returned BM25 score corresponding to b is treated as the value of b's BM25 feature.

- Hypernym translation (HT): Supposing the given English title is e and that e's hypernym is h, this feature is defined as the log frequency of h's Chinese translation in the candidate Chinese article.

- English translation occurrence (ETO): Whether or not w's title appears in the first sentence of b is regarded as the value of b's ETO feature.

After replicating Wang et al.'s (2014) system, we add our proposed cross-encyclopedia entity embedding (CEEE) feature, the construction of which is detailed in the following sections.

3.1 Cross-Encyclopedia Entity Embedding Model

Our model is based on Mikolov et al.'s (2013) skip-gram model. The training objective of the skip-gram model is to maximize the probability of predicting the target word given the context, where the target-context pairs are extracted by sliding a window over the entire corpus.

Within an online encyclopedia, each entity is linked with one or more other entities by hyperlinks. For example, the "Food" article in English Wikipedia is linked with the "Plant" article. On the assumption that the entities mentioned in an article are somehow related to the article's meaning, for a given context article, we treat all entities mentioned in it as target entities. Given a set of target-context entity pairs $E = \{(t, c)\}$, we learn the embeddings of entities by maximizing the training objective:

$$\mathcal{L} = \frac{1}{|E|}\Sigma_{(t,c)\in E}logP(t|c). \quad (1)$$

The probability of a target entity given a certain context entity is defined with the softmax function to represent the probability distribution over the entity space ε of an online encyclopedia:

$$P(t|c) = \frac{exp(v_t \odot v_c)}{\Sigma_{e\in\varepsilon}exp(v_e \odot v_c)} \quad (2)$$

, where $v_t, v_c \subset \mathbb{R}^d$ is the embedding of an entity, d is the embedding size and $\odot$ is dot product.

3.2 Learning Cross-Encyclopedia Entity Embedding

Since there are millions of entities in both Wikipedia and Baidu, we adopt negative sampling to speed up the training process. We set the negative sample size to 100 during training. We further filter out entities that are only linked to 9 or fewer other entities. We train the model with (1) Baidu as target and Wikipedia as context, (2) Wikipedia as target and Baidu as context, (3) Wikipedia as both target and context, and (4) Baidu as both target and context. During task (3), only m^w is updated, and during task (4), only m^b is updated. Every task iterates through its corresponding set of entity pairs. The four tasks repeat 50 times each. The embeddings are updated by stochastic gradient descent with a batch size of 1280 entity pairs. The learning rate is set to 0.1, and entity embeddings are randomly initialized. We also normalize the embeddings to the unit vector every 10 batches during training as Xing et al. (2015) did to improve entity similarity measurement.

3.3 Cross-Encyclopedia Entity Embedding Feature

After training, the learned embeddings are ready to be used. The similarity score of a Wikipedia entity and a Baidu entity is obtained by calculating the cosine value of their corresponding vectors in the learned embedding. Supposing the embedding vectors corresponding to the English Wikipedia article and the Baidu article are v_w and v_b, the feature value is defined as follows:

$$\begin{cases} \frac{v_w \cdot v_b}{|v_w||v_b|} & \text{if both } v_w \text{ and } v_b \text{ are available} \\ -1 & \text{otherwise} \end{cases} \quad (3)$$

4 Demo System

4.1 System Architecture

Our web-based demo system, Encyclolink, is composed of two modules: Web UI and Web Service. The Web UI is mainly written in simple HTML with CSS. The Web UI takes a user's input as the query. After receiving a query, the UI sends it to the Web Service with a JavaScript function. Then the Web Service will call our main CLAL module, described in Section 3, to retrieve and rank the candidate articles according to their scores. The flowchart of Encyclolink is depicted in Figure 1.

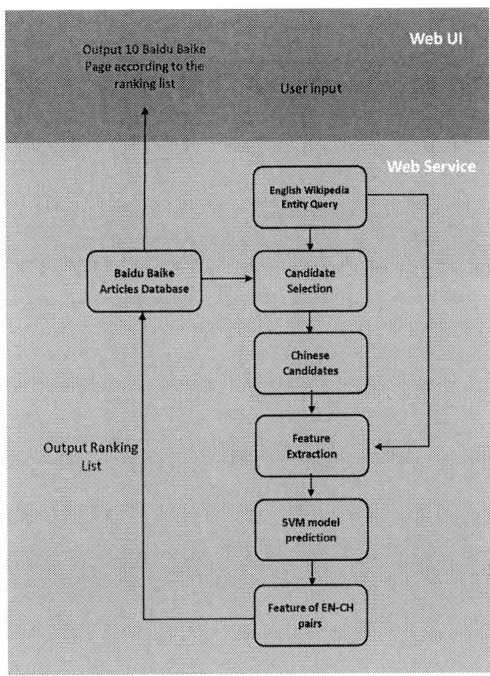

Figure 1: The flowchar of Encyclolink

4.2 User Interface and Application

The user interface of Encyclolink is separated into two main areas shown in Figure 2. The upper area contains a preview of the original English Wikipedia page. In the bottom area are the CLAL results given the input query. At the upper left corner of the UI screen, there is a text search field in which users can input a title of an article of interest. After the user presses the "Go" button, a preview of the English article will appear below the search field, including a hyperlink to the original English Wikipedia article. Meanwhile, the input query is sent to Web Service module, which selects and returns 10 candidate articles from Baidu Baike. They are listed in descending order according to their relevance scores to the query. Each of the candidates is also accompanied by a hyperlink, which users can click to open a window to view the contents of the Baidu Baike article. The UI allows users to view the English article alongside the corresponding Baidu Baike article on the same page for comparison.

5 Conclusion

This paper describes the Encyclolink system, a web-based system that can link articles from En-

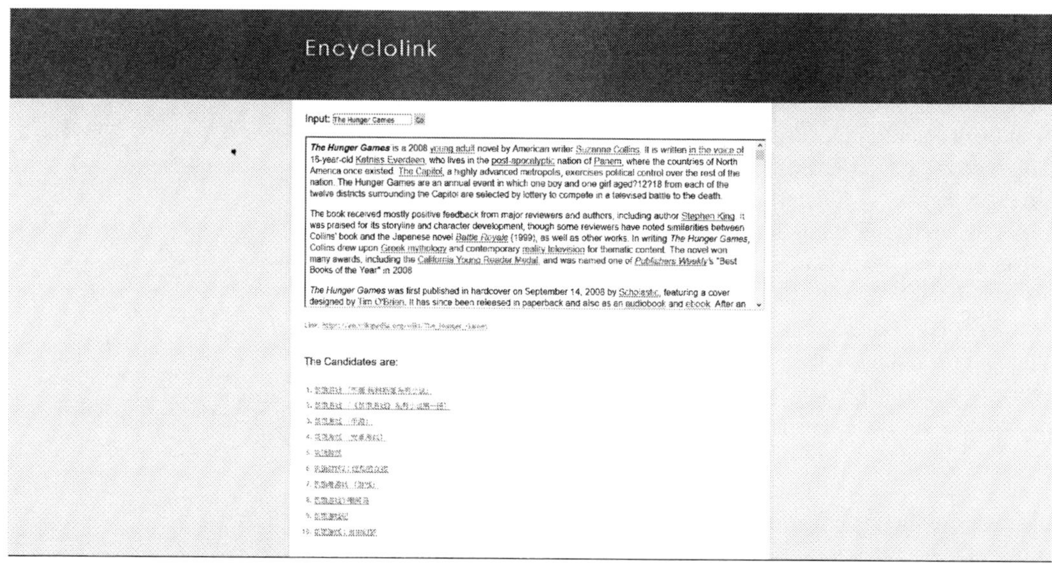

Figure 2: The Web UI of Encyclolink

glish Wikipedia and Chinese Baidu Baike, allowing users to retrieve and examine information from two of the world's largest online encyclopedias. A Encyclolink user can enter an English query to retrieve the matching English Wikipedia articles and a ranked list of corresponding Chinese articles in Baidu Baike. Encyclolink displays the results in a simple preview interface that lets users compare both English and Chinese encyclopedia articles side by side.

Acknowledgement

This research was supported in part by the Ministry of Science and Technology of Taiwan (MOST 104-2221-E-008-034-MY3), National Taiwan University (NTU-106R104045), Intel Corporation, and Delta Electronics, and Advantech.

References

Tomas Mikolov, Ilya Sutskever, Kai Chen, Greg S. Corrado, and Jeff Dean. 2013. Distributed representations of words and phrases and their compositionality. In *Proceedings of the 2013 Conference on Neural Information Processing Systems (NIPS)*. pages 3111–3119.

Jong-Hoon Oh, Daisuke Kawahara, Kiyotaka Uchimoto, Jun'ichi Kazama, and Kentaro Torisawa. 2008. Enriching multilingual language resources by discovering missing cross-language links in wikipedia. In *Proceedings of the 2008 IEEE/WIC/ACM International Conference on Web Intelligence and Intelligent Agent Technology*. volume 1, pages 322–328.

Philipp Sorg and Philipp Cimiano. 2008. Enriching the crosslingual link structure of wikipedia-a classification-based approach. In *Proceedings of the AAAI 2008 Workshop on Wikipedia and Artifical Intelligence*. pages 49–54.

Shyam Upadhyay, Manaal Faruqui, Chris Dyer, and Dan Roth. 2016. Cross-lingual models of word embeddings: An empirical comparison. In *Proceedings of the 54th Annual Meeting of the Association for Computational Linguistics (Volume 1: Long Papers)*. pages 1661–1670.

Yu-Chun Wang, Chun-Kai Wu, and Richard Tzong-Han Tsai. 2014. Cross-language and cross-encyclopedia article linking using mixed-language topic model and hypernym translation. In *Proceedings of the 52nd Annual Meeting of the Association for Computational Linguistics (Volume 2: Short Papers)*. Association for Computational Linguistics, pages 586–591.

Zhichun Wang, Juanzi Li, Zhigang Wang, and Jie Tang. 2012. Cross-lingual knowledge linking across wiki knowledge bases. In *Proceedings of the 21st international conference on World Wide Web*. pages 459–468.

Chao Xing, Dong Wang, Chao Liu, and Yiye Lin. 2015. Normalized word embedding and orthogonal transform for bilingual word translation. In *Proceedings of the 2015 Conference of the North American Chapter of the Association for Computational Linguistics: Human Language Technologies*. pages 1006–1011.

A Telecom-Domain Online Customer Service Assistant Based on Question Answering with Word Embedding and Intent Classification

Jui-Yang Wang[1], Ming-Feng Kuo[1], Jen-Chieh Han[1], Chao-Chuang Shih[1],
Chun-Hsun Chen[2], Po-Ching Lee[2], and Richard Tzong-Han Tsai[1,*]

[1]Department of Computer Science and Information Engineering,
National Central University, Taiwan, R.O.C.
[2]Telecommunication Laboratories,
Chunghwa Telecom Co., Ltd., Taiwan, R.O.C.
*corresponding author
thtsai@csie.ncu.edu.tw

Abstract

In the paper, we propose an information retrieval based (IR-based) Question Answering (QA) system to assist online customer service staffs respond users in the telecom domain. When user asks a question, the system retrieves a set of relevant answers and ranks them. Moreover, our system uses a novel reranker to enhance the ranking result of information retrieval. It employs the word2vec model to represent the sentences as vectors. It also uses a sub-category feature, predicted by the k-nearest neighbor algorithm. Finally, the system returns the top five candidate answers, making online staffs find answers much more efficiently.

1 Introduction

Online customer services have been used for decades. Providing the services with satisfactory quality requires a large number of well-trained online customer service staffs, making the cost not affordable for most companies. For online customer service staffs, the most time consuming tasks is to find appropriate answers from the log database of previous conversations or the frequently-asked-question database. Academic researchers and industrial engineers have made considerable efforts on developing automatic question-answering (QA) systems to support online customer services.

Currently, the most popular approach to find the answer given the queried question is information-retrieval-based. In this approach, the queried question is treated as a set of keywords. Then, these keywords are sent to an information retrieval engine, such as Apache Lucene[1], to search similar questions in the log or FAQ databases. All in-database questions are ranked according to their keyword-based similarities to the queried question. The main incapability of keyword-based similarity is that it considers only the appearance of surface keywords but overlooks the semantics. Thanks to the emergence of distributed representations of words (Mikolov et al., 2013), words are transformed to vectors that capture precise semantic word relationships. Therefore, the similarity between two questions could be measured in terms of their semantic meanings.

Currently, several studies have proved the effectiveness of incorporating word embedding features in answer ranking models (Zhou et al., 2015; Zhou and Huang, 2017; Belinkov et al., 2015; Tran et al., 2015). In our system, we derive our reranking model based on two SemEval-2016 studies (AlessandroMoschitti et al., 2016; Mihaylov and Nakov, 2016). We train a word embedding model to transform all questions into distributed vectors (Le and Mikolov, 2014; Dai et al., 2015). Due to every in-database question contains intention labels assigned by Chunghwa telecom customer service staffs, we train a multi-class classifier to identify the input questions intention. Finally, we design a reranking model using the word embedding features and the intention feature. Our system provides a web-based interface that present the user-staff conversation on the left pane and the candidate answers on the right pane, as shown in Figure 1.

---

[1]https://lucene.apache.org/

The Companion Volume of the IJCNLP 2017 Proceedings: System Demonstrations, pages 17–20,
Taipei, Taiwan, November 27 – December 1, 2017. ©2017 AFNLP

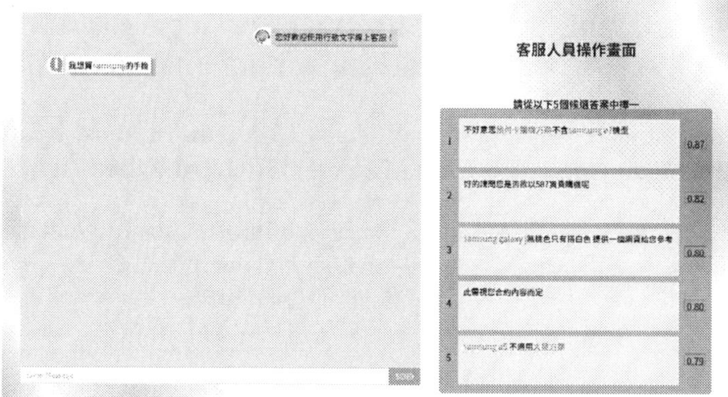

Figure 1: The user interface of our system. The dialogue part is on the left side, and the top 5 answers are beside it. Name entities in the answers are distinguished by different colors. The user in the figure types "I wants to buy a Samsung smartphone.". The responses are "I'm sorry. Samsung edge7 is not included in the prepaid card plan.", "OK. Are you going to buy cell phone the 587 plans?", "There is no Samsung galaxy j in Pink Gold. There is only white ones left. This is a web site that you can reference.", "It depends on your cell phone plan." and "Samsung a5 isn't included in the Dafa plan.".

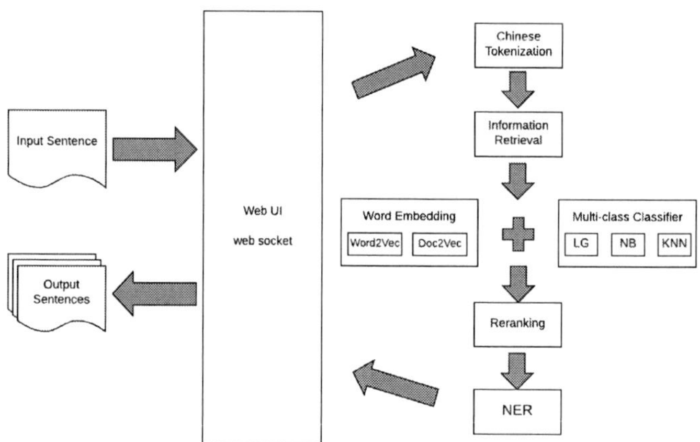

Figure 2: The architecture of our system

2 Architecture

In this section, we introduce the architecture of our system, as shown in Figure 2. Firstly, it pre-processes the input question and then retrieves top 100 QA pairs from the Chunghwa Telecom (CHT) customer-staff conversation log database. Then, our system employs a word embedding model to transform questions into vectors.

There are two models, Word2Vec[2] and Doc2Vec[3], to implement the word embedding. The word embedding make great result in finding the appropriate responses. To optimize the result,

we also do multi-class classification to obtain the category features of each pair. We compare different classifiers, logistic regression (LG), Naïve Bayes (NB) and k-nearest-neighbor (KNN). The system concatenates the results of Word2Vec, Doc2Vec and multi-class classification to be the feature of reranking. Finally, our system calculates the cosine similarity between the feature of the input query and the feature of QA pairs and choose the top 5 candidates. Additionally, the system recognizes the proper nouns in the output sentences and return the relevant information with the answers of top 5 candidates to the user. We will next detail each step in the following sections.

---

[2]https://radimrehurek.com/gensim/models/word2vec.html
[3]https://radimrehurek.com/gensim/models/doc2vec.html

2.1 Chinese Tokenization

Our system mainly used by the people who speak in Chinese, and Chinese words in the sentence don't have the labels to show the boundary between them. Thus, the system has to do the Chinese tokenization[4]. To solve the sequence labeling problem, people often utilize Hidden Markov Model (HMM) and Conditional Random Filed (CRF) because of their high accuracy. Our system should immediately realize the input messages. It also needs to update the new words and retraining the tokenizer regularly. As a result, we adopt HMM algorithm. It is fast, and it has high accuracy. It basically takes time to count the N-gram Frequency instead of modifying the weight of features, so its training time is far less than CRF.

2.2 Information Retrieval - Okapi BM25

For the information retrieval, we adopt the Okapi Best Matching 25 (BM25) algorithm. BM 25 is arguably one of the most important and widely used information retrieval function. It is effective and it has strong retrieval capacity. However, it lacks for variety, and it's hard to unite the properties of multiply entities.

2.3 Word2Vec

After the information retrieval, we take the top 100 entities to be the candidates. Each word in a candidate will be transformed into a fixed-length vector using Word2Vec model. Word2Vec is a high efficiency model using a real number vector to represent a word. It utilize the concept of deep learning, transforming the text into a k dimension vector through training. The similarity of the word vectors can represent the similarity of the words' semantic. Because sentences consist of words, we calculate the arithmetic mean of all word vectors in the same QA pair to represent the pair.

2.4 Doc2Vec

We have tried another word embedding model, Doc2Vec, to map the sentences to unique vectors as well. Doc2Vec's concept is alike to Word2Vec except the additional paragraph vector. The paragraph vector represents the missing information from the current context and can act as a memory of the topic of the paragraph. Word2Vec and Doc2Vec can effectively make the inappropriate candidates' rank drop and left the good answers in

the top 5 order. Besides being a feature to rerank the 100 pairs, the result of Doc2Vec is also the input feature of multi-class classification which is discussed in next section.

2.5 Intention Prediction

The intention of the input question is effective for searching similar question to it. For example, the question "How to renew my plan for acquiring an iphone 7" is similar to "I want to buy an iphone 7, could you suggest me a suitable plan?" Word-based similarity measures are hard to detect their similarity because they have few words in common. However, incorporating intention information could mitigate this problem. Fortunately, every question in the CHT customer-staff conversation log database has intention labels. Therefore, we could train a multi-class classification model to predict the intention label. We have tried three modes: logistic regression, Naïve Bayes and k-nearest-neighbor. The results will be presented in Section 3.1

2.6 NER

The contents of the answers usually contain many proper nouns such as plans, devices, Store location, etc. To respond to the user, we need the information of them. Consequently, it is important to distinguish which word is a proper noun. We use CRF Model to address the problem and train several models for the name of special offers, product name, location. The accuracy is 91%, 71.4%, 85.86%, respectively. We design the features like the suffix, brand name, product id, etc. The training data is the CHT dialogue corpus and some data collected from sogi[5].

3 Experiment and Results

3.1 Intention Prediction

In this section, we compare the different classifiers, logistic regression, Naïve Bayes and KNN. The training data is CHT dialogue corpus. It consists of 113425 sentences classified in 10 categories by the customer service staff in CHT. However, it contains a lot of noisy data which impact the performances. We manually select the most common 120 sentences in each category to be the test data, and there are 1200 sentences in total. Table 1 shows the comparison of different mod-

---

[4]https://github.com/fxsjy/jieba

[5]https://www.sogi.com.tw/

els. Using Doc2vec vector as feature, KNN significantly outperform other classifiers.

Type of Classifier	Pre.	Rec.	F-1
Logistic Regression	0.61	0.62	0.6
Gaussian Naïve Bayes	0.61	0.5	0.48
Bernoulli Naïve Bayes	0.52	0.45	0.44
K-Nearest Neighbor	**0.72**	**0.62**	**0.63**

Table 1: Comparison of different classifiers on the test data.

3.2 Reranker

To validate our approach, our system compares with the baseline, BM25, implemented in Solr. The test data is the most common query in each category. It retrieves 100 QA pairs per query. We evaluate the result of reranking using Mean Average Precision (MAP) of top 5 candidates and all candidates respectively. Table 2 and Table 3 show the performance of the experiments. Different word embedding models have different advantages. The average of Word2Vec vectors contains semantic information. Doc2vec vectors extract syntactic information from sentences. Moreover, multi-class classifiers aid to identify the categories of sentences.

Method	MAP
BM25	0.9197
Word2Vec	0.9671
Word2Vec + Doc2Vec	0.9692
Word2Vec + Doc2Vec + KNN	1

Table 2: MAP of top 5 QA pairs in different method.

Method	MAP
BM25	0.7034
Word2Vec	0.7774
Word2Vec + Doc2Vec	0.8198
Word2Vec + Doc2Vec + KNN	0.8279

Table 3: MAP of all candidate QA pairs in different method.

4 Conclusion

We present a novel system to economizes on manpower and material resources in the the online customer service. It outperforms the famous information retrieval algorithm through word representation and multi-class classification, and it achieves excellent performance.

Although there are many NN-based technique in our system, some components still need to be improved. For example, attention LSTM model shows that it's effective to know the focus word in the sentence. Therefore, we could use it to deal with intention prediction. In the reranker component, the answer part in a QA pair has not been used to match the input question in our module. The answer part plays an important role that we can use neural network to learn. These directions are worthy of our in-depth study in the future.

References

PreslavNakov LluısMarquez AlessandroMoschitti, WalidMagdy HamdyMubarak AbedAlhakim-Freihat, James Glass, and Bilal Randeree. 2016. Semeval-2016 task 3: Community question answering. *Proceedings of SemEval*, pages 525–545.

Yonatan Belinkov, Mitra Mohtarami, Scott Cyphers, and James R Glass. 2015. Vectorslu: A continuous word vector approach to answer selection in community question answering systems. In *SemEval@ NAACL-HLT*, pages 282–287.

Andrew M Dai, Christopher Olah, and Quoc V Le. 2015. Document embedding with paragraph vectors. *arXiv preprint arXiv:1507.07998*.

Quoc Le and Tomas Mikolov. 2014. Distributed representations of sentences and documents. In *Proceedings of the 31st International Conference on Machine Learning (ICML-14)*, pages 1188–1196.

Todor Mihaylov and Preslav Nakov. 2016. Semanticz at semeval-2016 task 3: Ranking relevant answers in community question answering using semantic similarity based on fine-tuned word embeddings. In *SemEval@ NAACL-HLT*, pages 879–886.

Tomas Mikolov, Ilya Sutskever, Kai Chen, Greg S Corrado, and Jeff Dean. 2013. Distributed representations of words and phrases and their compositionality. In *Advances in neural information processing systems*, pages 3111–3119.

Quan Hung Tran, Vu Tran, Tu Vu, Minh Nguyen, and Son Bao Pham. 2015. Jaist: Combining multiple features for answer selection in community question answering. In *SemEval@ NAACL-HLT*, pages 215–219.

Guangyou Zhou, Tingting He, Jun Zhao, and Po Hu. 2015. Learning continuous word embedding with metadata for question retrieval in community question answering. In *ACL (1)*, pages 250–259.

Guangyou Zhou and Jimmy Xiangji Huang. 2017. Modeling and learning distributed word representation with metadata for question retrieval. *IEEE Transactions on Knowledge and Data Engineering*, 29(6):1226–1239.

TOTEMSS: <u>T</u>opic-based, <u>T</u>emporal <u>S</u>entiment <u>S</u>ummarisation for Twitter

Bo Wang[1], Maria Liakata[1,2], Adam Tsakalidis[1], Spiros Georgakopoulos Kolaitis[1],
Symeon Papadopoulos[3], Lazaros Apostolidis[3], Arkaitz Zubiaga[1], Rob Procter[1,2]
Yiannis Kompatsiaris[3]
[1] University of Warwick, UK
[2] The Alan Turing Institute, London, UK
[3] Information Technologies Institute (ITI), CERTH, Greece
{bo.wang, a.tsakalidis, m.liakata}@warwick.ac.uk

Abstract

We present a system for time-sensitive, topic-based summarisation of sentiment around target entities and topics in collections of tweets. We describe the main elements of the system and present two examples of sentiment analysis of topics related to the 2017 UK general election.

1 Introduction

In recent years social media such as Twitter have gained prominence as a rich resource for opinion mining and sentiment analysis on diverse topics. However, analysing sentiment about diverse topics and how it evolves over time in large volumes of tweets is a difficult task. In this paper, we present a system for analysing sentiment about specific topics or entities over time while providing fine-grained summaries to give insights into the underlying reasons. We illustrate its use with examples of topics discussed on Twitter during the 2017 UK general election.

Our problem formulation is related to work on prospective information needs, represented by the Microblog (Lin et al., 2015), Temporal Summarisation (Aslam et al., 2015) and Real-Time Summarisation (Lin et al., 2016) tracks at recent Text Retrieval Conferences (TRECs). However, while the aim of these tasks is to keep users up-to-date with topics of interest via push notifications or email digests, our aim is to provide an interactive user interface that shows how sentiment towards specific entities or topics develops over time. We have incorporated an automatic summarisation feature to assist users in understanding the underlying reasons. Thus, our motivation is related to the one discussed in (Meng et al., 2012), which also proposes a topic-oriented opinion summarisation framework. However, we use state-of-the-art methods enabling intuitive and interactive visualisation of sentiments in chronological order. This provides a useful tool for analysing an important event over time, such as elections, both quantitatively and qualitatively.

Here, we describe our system that aims at the aforementioned objectives. Its interactive web interface is accessible online[1]. We also present two use cases to demonstrate how the system can be used in analysing public sentiment.

2 System Design

An overview of the system is depicted in Figure 1 and comprises: 1) Data collection and sampling; 2) Sentiment classification; 3) Tweet summarisation; and 4) Data visualisation.

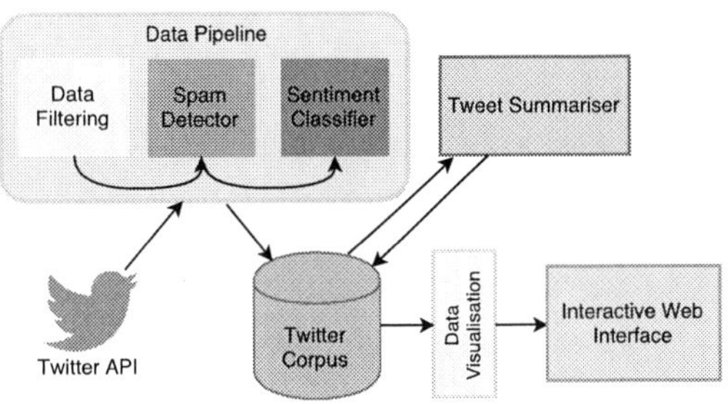

Figure 1: System overview.

2.1 Data Collection and Sampling

We collected a corpus of tweets about the 2017 UK general election through Twitter's streaming API by tracking 15 hashtags[2]. Data harvesting was performed between 26 May and 21 June 2017

---

[1] Live demo: `http://bit.ly/2g5lBcH`

[2] #ukelection2017, #ge2017, #ge17, #ukge2017, #ukgeneralelection2017, #bbcqt, #bbcdp, #marrshow, #generalelection2017, #generalelection, #electionuk, #ukelection, #electionuk2017 and #brexit

The Companion Volume of the IJCNLP 2017 Proceedings: System Demonstrations, pages 21–24,
Taipei, Taiwan, November 27 – December 1, 2017. ©2017 AFNLP

to capture discussions in the two weeks running up to and after the election. To identify relevant topics and entities in each tweet, we match tweets against two manually curated lists of keywords (both were created during the 2015 UK election cycle) which include 438 topic keywords relevant to nine popular election issues (e.g., immigration, NHS) and a list of 71 political party aliases (e.g. 'tories', 'lib dems'). The resulting corpus contains 3,663,090 tweets, with each tweet mentioning at least one keyword. To increase data quality and reduce noise in the corpus, we trained and applied a Twitter spam detection model using features described in (Wang et al., 2015).

2.2 Sentiment Classification

Jiang et al. (2011) showed that 40% of Twitter sentiment classification errors are caused by tweet-level approaches that disregard topics/entities. We go beyond tweet-level approaches and adopt the multi-target-specific approach proposed in (Wang et al., 2017b), which finds the syntactically connected parts of a tweet associated with each topic or entity, and extracts word embedding features from them to classify sentiment as 'negative', 'positive' or 'neutral'. This approach obtained state-of-the-art performance in both single- and multi-target benchmark data sets (Wang et al., 2017b). The whole data pipeline of Figure 1 is designed to dispatch work to many machines in parallel[3], processing many data batches simultaneously, which makes it very fast.

2.3 Tweet Summarisation

Here we aim to extract a list of representative tweets summarising the sentiment(s) expressed towards each topic/entity on each day (e.g. tweets containing positive sentiment towards 'NHS' posted on 26 June 2017).

As a prerequisite for summarisation, we group tweets containing the same sentiment towards a topic/entity on a day into a number of clusters, with each cluster assumed to represent a common theme or reason underlying the particular choice of sentiment. We adopt the two-stage hierarchical topic modelling approach proposed in (Wang et al., 2017a) and select the GSDMM+OLDA model for this task due to its effectiveness and efficiency. If there are fewer than 10 unique tweets containing the same sentiment towards a topic (or entity) on a particular day, we skip clustering and treat each of these tweets as a cluster.

To extract representative tweets summarising each cluster, we place every tweet in one common embedding space and identify 20 tweets closest to the cluster centroid (also known as metroid tweets) as summary candidates. The embedding space here is constructed using a simple but effective sentence embedding method proposed by Arora et al. (2017), which reported good performance on 22 textual similarity data sets, including a Twitter corpus. We then rank the 20 summary candidates based on weighted average tf-idf scores in the cluster; these scores can be regarded as a measure of informativeness.

We select the most informative tweet from the 20 candidates as the summary for that cluster and the final summary for the sentiment expressed towards the topic/entity is the combination of all its cluster summaries (e.g., tweets containing positive sentiment towards 'NHS' posted on 26 June 2017, comprise 8 clusters, each summarised by a single informative tweet).

2.4 Data Visualisation

For each topic/entity we calculate the following daily features: *# of tweets, # of unique users, # of tweets per sentiment type (pos, neg, neutral)* and *# of unique users per sentiment*. These features were selected on the basis of previous work on election prediction with social media (Tsakalidis et al., 2015). These are accompanied by the daily summaries of each sentiment type for a given topic/entity as described above.

In addition to showing the raw values of the above features, we also normalised sentiment features (*# of tweets per sentiment, # of unique users per sentiment*) to reflect the percentage of sentiment of a particular type towards a topic/entity on a particular day. To allow time series comparisons across different topics/entities we normalised the *# of tweets* and *# of unique users* of all topics/entities across all days in the range [0, 1]. Finally, to account for differences in popularity, we calculated the average (per-topic and across all days) *# of tweets* and *# of unique users*.

The web interface is implemented on Web standards (HTML5/CSS3). The timeline graphs are built using the NVD3[4] library (reusable charts for `d3.js`), while the auto-complete function-

---

[3]We ran it on a server with 40 CPU cores and 64 GB of RAM.

[4]http://nvd3.org/

ality is based on the 'Ajax AutoComplete for jQuery' library[5]. In addition, jQuery from Google Hosted Libraries[6] and D3.js from Cloudfare Hosted Libraries[7] are used for DOM manipulation (add/remove elements, click events, etc.) and accessing data (from tsv files) respectively.

3 Example Use Cases

We use two use cases to demonstrate how our system can help analyse public sentiment on Twitter.

3.1 Use Case #1 – Party Sentiment

Recent election campaigns suggest that the Twittersphere tends to contain more negative sentiment during the election period. Hence, in the first case study, we compare negative sentiment trends on Twitter for the two major UK political parties, 'Conservative' and 'Labour', before and after the 2017 UK general election. As described in section 2.4, the negative sentiment reflects the percentage of negative sentiment for each party on each day over all sentiment bearing tweets.

Figure 2 reveals consistently more negative sentiment towards 'Conservative' than 'Labour', especially for the week before election day (8 June).

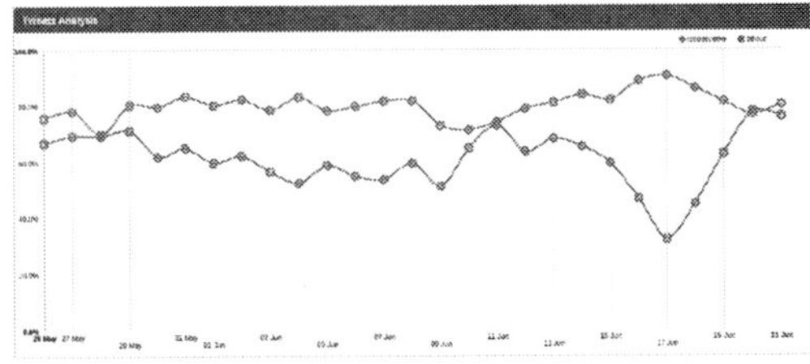

Figure 2: Negative sentiment trends for 'Labour' (red) and 'Conservative' (blue).

3.2 Use Case #2 – Grenfell Tower Fire

To provide deeper insight into the advantages of our opinion summarisation system, we present a case study on how public sentiment towards the topic 'housing' developed before and after the Grenfell Tower Fire disaster[8]. Figure 3 shows the percentage of users expressing negative sentiment towards 'housing' as well as the governing party 'conservative' over the period covering the incident. Our web interface allows users to click on each circle shown on the graph to display tweet summaries for that topic on that particular day.

We can see the number of users expressing negative sentiment for the topic 'housing' fluctuated throughout the election period while it remained fairly constant for 'Conservative'. Negative sentiment peaked in both cases on June 16th.

Table 1 presents a negative sentiment summary for each day between June 12 and 15, and all three negative opinion summary tweets on the peak day of June 16 showing each summary tweet represents a different aspect of the topic. Along with the graph shown in Figure 3, this summary offers a tight integration of topic, sentiment and insight into reasons behind the sentiment. Before the fire, negative sentiment towards 'housing' was austerity related; after the fire, the incident dominated the 'housing' discussion on Twitter. A large portion of users blame the Conservative government for the decline of social housing and ultimately the Grenfell Tower fire. Finally, on June 16 each of the negative opinion summaries represents one theme related to this topic, namely 'the decline of social housing', 'immigration and housing' and 'the votes on housing safety'.

4 Conclusion

We presented a monitoring system for topic-entity sentiment on Twitter that summarises public opinion around the sentiment towards each entity. The system deployment for the 2017 UK election, provides an interactive visualisation for comparing sentiment trends and display opinion summaries on the graph. In the future, we plan to improve our system to produce more concise summaries and allow near real-time processing of new events.

References

Sanjeev Arora, Yingyu Liang, and Tengyu Ma. 2017. A simple but tough-to-beat baseline for sentence embeddings. In *Proceedings of the 5th International Conference on Learning Representations (ICLR)*.

Javed Aslam, Fernando Diaz, Matthew Ekstrand-Abueg, Richard McCreadie, Virgil Pavlu, and Tetsuya Sakai. 2015. Trec 2015 temporal summarization track overview. In *Proceedings of the 24th Text REtrieval Conference, TREC*.

Long Jiang, Mo Yu, Ming Zhou, Xiaohua Liu, and Tiejun Zhao. 2011. Target-dependent twitter senti-

---

[5] https://www.devbridge.com/sourcery/
components/jquery-autocomplete/
[6] https://developers.google.com/speed/
libraries/
[7] https://cdnjs.com/
[8] https://en.wikipedia.org/wiki/Grenfell_
Tower_fire

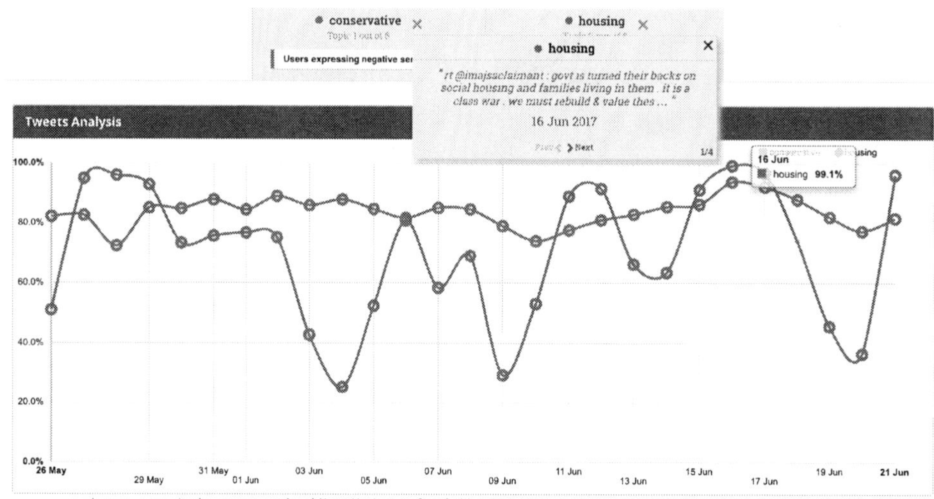

Figure 3: Negative sentiment trends for 'housing' (red) and 'conservative' (blue), with a summary tweet displayed for the former.

Topic entity	Opinion Summaries	Date
housing	rt @user1 : the audacity to even refer to tackling a " housing crisis " after being in government for 7 years . https://t.co/lifwybhryp	12 June 2017
housing	austerity is still here , bedroom tax , foodbanks , pip , housing cap , universal credit taper , welfare freeze , esa cuts , inflation is up . #ge17	13 June 2017
housing	@bbcnews @skynews @itvnews tories cuts in society kill just look at social housing #grenfelltower sold to cheapest bidding #ge17 #bbcqt	14 June 2017
housing	tory capitalism cutting kills social housing on the cheap #grenfelltower cuts in fire ambulance police nhs services #victorialive #ge17	15 June 2017
housing	rt @user2 : govt is turned their backs on social housing and families living in them . it is a class war . we must rebuild & value thes ...	16 June 2017
housing	rt @user3 : laura perrins again blaming the death toll of #grenfelltower on immigration - putting pressure on housing . laura bt ...	16 June 2017
housing	rt @user4 : it is a shame the ministers hearts did not go out to the people in grenfell tower when they were voting on housing safety #bbcqt	16 June 2017

Table 1: Negative opinion summary for 'housing' before and after the Grenfell Tower fire

ment classification. In *Proceedings of the 49th Annual Meeting of the Association for Computational Linguistics.*

Jimmy Lin, Miles Efron, Yulu Wang, Garrick Sherman, and Ellen Voorhees. 2015. Overview of the trec-2015 microblog track. In *Proceedings of the 24th Text REtrieval Conference, TREC.*

Jimmy Lin, Adam Roegiest, Luchen Tan, Richard Mc-Creadie, Ellen Voorhees, and Fernando Diaz. 2016. Overview of the trec 2016 real-time summarization track. In *Proceedings of the 25th Text REtrieval Conference, TREC*, volume 16.

Xinfan Meng, Furu Wei, Xiaohua Liu, Ming Zhou, Sujian Li, and Houfeng Wang. 2012. Entity-centric topic-oriented opinion summarization in twitter. In *Proceedings of the 18th ACM SIGKDD.*

Adam Tsakalidis, Symeon Papadopoulos, Alexandra I Cristea, and Yiannis Kompatsiaris. 2015. Predicting elections for multiple countries using twitter and polls. *IEEE Intelligent Systems*, 30(2):10–17.

Bo Wang, Maria Liakata, Arkaitz Zubiaga, and Rob Procter. 2017a. A hierarchical topic modelling approach for tweet clustering. In *Proceedings of the 9th International Conference on Social Informatics (SocInfo).*

Bo Wang, Maria Liakata, Arkaitz Zubiaga, and Rob Procter. 2017b. Tdparse-multi-target-specific sentiment recognition on twitter. In *Proceedings of the 15th Conference of the European Chapter of the Association for Computational Linguistics.*

Bo Wang, Arkaitz Zubiaga, Maria Liakata, and Rob Procter. 2015. Making the most of tweet-inherent features for social spam detection on twitter. In *5th Workshop on Making Sense of Microposts (#Microposts2015) WWW*, volume 1395, pages 10–16.

MUSST: A Multilingual Syntactic Simplification Tool

Carolina Scarton and **Lucia Specia**
University of Sheffield
Sheffield, UK

Alessio Palmero Aprosio and **Sara Tonelli**
Fondazione Bruno Kessler
Trento, Italy

Tamara Martín Wanton
H.I. IBERIA
Madrid, Spain

Abstract

We describe MUSST, a multilingual syntactic simplification tool. The tool supports sentence simplifications for English, Italian and Spanish, and can be easily extended to other languages. Our implementation includes a set of general-purpose simplification rules, as well as a sentence selection module (to select sentences to be simplified) and a confidence model (to select only promising simplifications). The tool was implemented in the context of the European project SIMPATICO on text simplification for Public Administration (PA) texts. Our evaluation on sentences in the PA domain shows that we obtain correct simplifications for 76% of the simplified cases in English, 71% of the cases in Spanish. For Italian, the results are lower (38%) but the tool is still under development.

1 Introduction

Text simplification is the task of reducing the lexical and/or syntactic complexity of a text (Siddharthan, 2004). It is common to divide this task in two subtasks: lexical simplification (LS) and syntactic simplification (SS). Whilst LS deals with the identification and replacement of difficult words or phrases, SS focuses on making complex syntactic constructions simpler. It is known, for instance, that passive voice constructions are more complex than active voice, and that long sentences with multiple clauses are more difficult to be understood than short sentences with a single clause. Several tools have been developed for LS (Paetzold and Specia, 2016). However, we are not aware of freely available tools for SS.

The SIMPATICO project[1] addresses text simplification for specific target audiences and domains. The project has three use cases focusing on different audiences: non-native speakers (Sheffield, UK), elderly (Galicia, Spain) and business and general citizens (Trento, Italy). Although personalised simplifications for each user type is our ultimate goal, we lack user-specific data. Therefore, our first step was to design general-purpose simplification rules which will later be specialised for the domain under consideration (PA). This solution led to the development of MUSST, which includes SS modules for three languages.

MUSST is based on the framework proposed by Siddharthan (2004) and is available as an open source Python implementation. Our rules split conjoint clauses, relative clauses and appositive phrases, and change sentences from passive into active voice. These are arguably the most widely applicable simplification operations across languages. We use the Stanford dependency parser (Chen and Manning, 2014) for the three languages, which enabled us to build a consistent multilingual tool. MUSST is evaluated using corpora extracted from the SIMPATICO use cases data. Such corpora (one for each language) were checked and – where applicable – syntactically simplified by experts in the area.

Inspired by the work of Gasperin et al. (2009), we also developed a complexity checker module in order to select sentences that should be simplified. In addition, we implemented a confidence model in order to predict whether or not a simplification produced by MUSST is good enough to be shown to the end-user. Developing these two modules required small labelled training sets.

To the best of our knowledge, MUSST is the

---

[1] https://www.simpatico-project.eu/

25

The Companion Volume of the IJCNLP 2017 Proceedings: System Demonstrations, pages 25–28,
Taipei, Taiwan, November 27 – December 1, 2017. ©2017 AFNLP

first freely available, open-source tool for SS in three languages, which – because of its modular nature – can be extended to other languages using the same framework.

2 Architecture

The architecture of MUSST has three main modules: analysis, transformation and generation (Siddharthan, 2004).

2.1 *Analysis*

The *Analysis* module is responsible for processing sentences to search for clues for the simplification of conjoint clauses (discourse markers) and relative clauses (relative pronouns). Sentences where cues are found trigger dedicated functions of the *Transformation* module.

Discourse markers need to be classified according to their semantics, in order to be correctly handled by the simplification rules. For instance, a conjoint clause with "and" as discourse marker should be processed differently from a conjoint clause with "when" as a discourse marker.

At this stage, the only mandatory text pre-processing steps are tokenization, which is done using the Stanford dependency parser, and lower-casing, which is done using the built-in function `lower()` in Python.

2.2 *Transformation*

In the *Transformation* module, our rules that simplify conjoint clauses, relative clauses, appositive phrases and passive voice are applied. This module is the core of MUSST. The main method is called `simplify`, which receives a sentence as input and returns one or more simplified sentences. The simplification is implemented as a recursive process that will keep simplifying the sentence until there is no more simplification rule that applies. The order of simplification is: appositive phrases, conjoint clauses, relative clauses and passive voice. This order has been defined empirically.

All the simplifications are done based on the output of the dependency parsers. For English and Spanish, we used the parsers available in CoreNLP[2], trained with Universal Dependencies[3] datasets. For Italian, we used the parser available

in Tint[4] (Palmero Aprosio and Moretti, 2016) (an adapted version of CoreNLP for Italian).

Figure 1 shows the parser output for the sentence "These organisations have been checked by us and should provide you with a quality service.", as an example. The sentence is first sent to the *Analysis* module that will search for discourse markers. In this case, "and" is found and the sentence is thus sent to the conjoint clauses rule. Such a rule searches for two tags in the root dependencies: ADVL (adverbial clause modifier) or CC (coordinating conjugation). In our example, there is a CC relation between "checked" (the root) and "and". Since "and" is on the list of markers in the *Analysis* module, the next step is to search for a CONJ (conjunction) tag. In the example, there is a CONJ relation between "checked" and "provide". The conjoint clause rule is then applied and the sentence is split into two. Each sentence is then sent to the *Generation* module. The simplified sentence at this stage is "These organisations have been checked by us. And these organisations should provide you with a quality service." Then, each of these simplified sentences are sent again to the simplifier in a recursive manner.

```
det(organisations-2, These-1)
nsubjpass(checked-5, organisations-2)
aux(checked-5, have-3)
auxpass(checked-5, been-4)
root(ROOT-0, checked-5)
case(us-7, by-6)
nmod(checked-5, us-7)
cc(checked-5, and-8)
aux(provide-10, should-9)
conj(checked-5, provide-10)
dobj(provide-10, you-11)
case(service-15, with-12)
det(service-15, a-13)
compound(service-15, quality-14)
nmod(provide-10, service-15)
```

Figure 1: Example of parser output.

The *Transformation* module is also responsible for sending the *Generation* module all the information needed for re-generating the simplified sentences. This information includes: discourse marker, relative pronoun, PoS tag of main and modal verbs and PoS tag of subject.

2.3 *Generation*

This module is responsible for re-constructing the simplified sentence(s) and guaranteeing that gram-

[2]`http://stanfordnlp.github.io/CoreNLP/`
[3]`http://universaldependencies.org`
[4]`http://tint.fbk.eu/parsing.html`

maticality is preserved. It needs to account for the fact that a sentence can be split (conjoint and relative clauses and appositive phrases) or reordered (passive voice).

Truecasing and removal of extra punctuation are also implemented in this module. For truecasing, we call a Python implementation that has a pre-trained model for English[5], and train truecasing models using monolingual corpora for Spanish and Italian. For punctuation removal we use rules that identify punctuation repetition.

In the case of conjoint clauses, we may need to add specific discourse markers to the simplified sentences depending on the markers in the original one. For example, if the complex discourse marker is "although", the second simplified sentence will start with "but".

For appositive phrases, the verb that connects the subject to the apposition is defined according to the number of the subject and the tense of the main verb. For instance, the simplified version of "Truffles, a luxury food, are delicious." is "Truffles are delicious. Truffles are a luxury food.".

Changes in passive voice also require verb changes. Such changes need to respect the tense of the verb and the person number of the subject. Changes in the pronoun realisation are also modelled: when pronouns are the subject of the passive voice, they will become the object of the verb in active voice.For verb conjugation we use the NodeBox toolkit[6] for English and the tool for verb conjugation in Tint for Italian. For Spanish, we developed a new module.

No further treatment is needed for relative clauses.

3 Evaluation

For English, we selected $1,100$ sentences from the Sheffield City Council website[7]. Such sentences were processed by MUSST, which led to 292 simplified sentences. We categorised these simplified sentences depending on whether or not they were correct simplifications (according to grammar). From the 292 sentences, 70 sentences were considered incorrect. Errors are usually created from parser issues. For instance, the sentence "PE kit, school bag, packed lunch." was incorrectly simplified to "PE kit packed lunch. PE kit

was school bag.". The dependency parser identified "packed" as the main verb, so the appositive phrase rule was applied. Since such problems are difficult to detect during simplification, we suggest using a confidence model (Section 4.2) after simplification.

For Italian, on a test set of 263 Italian sentences from SIMPITIKI corpus (Tonelli et al., 2016), 92 were simplified by MUSST. 57 of these sentences were judged as incorrect simplifications. The major cause of problems is also parsing errors, especially when sentences are particularly long or have ambiguous connectives.

For Spanish, out of 73 sentences from the Xunta Galicia website[8], 49 sentences were simplified by MUSST. Only 14 of these sentences were considered incorrect and the main issues were also due to parsing errors.

4 Extra modules

4.1 Complexity checker

Gasperin et al. (2009) proposes a binary classifier to decide whether or not a sentence should be split. We build a similar but more general classifier to decide whether a sentence should be simplified (including passive to active voice simplification).

We use the Naive Bayes implementation from the scikit-learn toolkit[9] to train a classifier with 10-fold cross-validation[10]. As features, we extracted simple counts of content words, syllables, tokens and punctuation along with number of clauses, discourse markers and relative pronouns.

For English, we used the $1,100$ sentences presented in Section 3. For Italian, we used a set of 405 sentences from SIMPITIKI and, for Spanish, we used a set of 104 sentences from the Xunta de Galicia website. All these sentences had been manually checked and – where applicable – simplified by experts, so each simplified sentence was considered a positive example.

Table 1 shows the performance of our classifiers in terms of precision, recall, F1 score and accuracy. All languages outperform the *majority class* classifiers in terms of accuracy (values in brackets), even though we rely on simple features and small training sets. The best F1 was achieved by the model for Spanish, closely followed by the model for English. Although the model for Italian

---

[5] https://github.com/nreimers/truecaser
[6] https://www.nodebox.net/code/index.php/Linguistics
[7] https://www.sheffield.gov.uk/

[8] http://www.xunta.gal/portada/
[9] http://scikit-learn.org/
[10] Other algorithms performed worse.

```
cscarton:simpatico_ss$ python __main__.py -l en -d ../tests/examples.en.toy -comp -conf
These organisations have been checked by us and should provide you with a quality service.
Suppose you later have a problem and need to use your contingency money . Then you can contact our customer accounts team to explain why you need this money .
The U.S. price is currently 18 cents a pound .  The U.S. price runs well above the world rate . So the 23,403 tons are still a lucrative target for growers .
The 23,403 tons are three quarters of the share .
If people have got in place proper effective safety measures, then naturally we are pleased about that.
Although both India and Pakistan announced troop withdrawals along the border, they both left their forces in Kashmir intact.
```

Figure 2: Example of MUSST usage.

has the best precision, its recall is the worst. The model for English has the lowest precision, but the highest recall. The Spanish model has similar values for precision and recall.

	F1	Precision	Recall	Accuracy
English	0.61	0.56	0.68	0.81 (0.78)
Italian	0.60	0.63	0.57	0.66 (0.58)
Spanish	0.62	0.61	0.62	0.76 (0.70)

Table 1: Performance of the complexity checkers.

4.2 Confidence model

In order to decide whether the simplified version of a sentence is "good enough" for a user, we trained a confidence model to classify a simplification as acceptable or not. Using the 292 sentences simplified by the English system and evaluated in Section 3, we built a confidence model for this language. The 70 sentences classified as incorrect (Section 3) were used as negative examples, whilst the remaining sentences received the positive label.

As features, we used the same basic counts as for the complexity checker (Section 4.1) along with language model (LM) probabilities and perplexity and grammar checking on the simplifications. KenLM[11] (Heafield, 2011) was used to extract LM features. A Python grammar checker was used for evaluating grammaticality[12]. The model was trained using the Random Forest implementation from scikit-learn with 10-fold cross-validation and achieved 0.80 of accuracy (F1/Precision/recall = 0.60/0.69/0.53), outperforming the MC classifier (accuracy = 0.61).

For Italian and Spanish, we also experimented with the datasets presented in Section 3, but the performance is worse because of the significantly smaller training sets. Nevertheless, both models outperform the majority class baseline in terms of accuracy. For Italian, our model achieved 0.80 of accuracy, against 0.66 for the majority class baseline. For Spanish, our model achieved 0.73 of accuracy (baseline = 0.55).

5 Demo outline

MUSST is available for download at `https://github.com/SIMPATICOProject/SimpaticoTAEServer/tree/ijcnlp2017-demo`. During the demo session we will present simplifications using both the command line (e.g. as in Figure 2) and the graphical interface of the SIMPATICO Dashboard (`http://simpatico.fbk.eu/demo2/webdemo/index.html`). We will demonstrate the use of `-comp` and `-conf` parameters that activate the complexity checker and confidence model, respectively.

Finally, we will discuss how a new language can be included into the tool.

Acknowledgments

This work has been supported by the European Commission project SIMPATICO (H2020-EURO-6-2015, grant number 692819).

References

D. Chen and C. D. Manning. 2014. A fast and accurate dependency parser using neural networks. In *EMNLP 2014*.

C. Gasperin, L. Specia, T. F. Pereira, and S. M. Aluísio. 2009. Learning when to simplify sentences for natural text simplification. In *ENIA 2009*.

K. Heafield. 2011. KenLM: Faster and Smaller Language Model Queries. In *WMT 2011*.

G. H. Paetzold and L. Specia. 2016. Benchmarking Lexical Simplification Systems. In *LREC 2016*.

A. Palmero Aprosio and G. Moretti. 2016. Italy goes to Stanford: a collection of CoreNLP modules for Italian. *ArXiv e-prints*.

A. Siddharthan. 2004. *Syntactic simplification and text cohesion*. Ph.D. thesis, University of Cambridge.

S. Tonelli, A. Palmero Aprosio, and F. Saltori. 2016. SIMPITIKI: a Simplification corpus for Italian extracted from Wikipedia. In *CLiC-it 2016*.

---

[11] `https://github.com/kpu/kenlm`
[12] `https://pypi.python.org/pypi/grammar-check/`

XMU Neural Machine Translation Online Service

Boli Wang, Zhixing Tan, Jinming Hu, Yidong Chen and **Xiaodong Shi**[*]

School of Information Science and Engineering, Xiamen University, Fujian, China

{boliwang, playinf, todtom}@stu.xmu.edu.cn

{ydchen, mandel}@xmu.edu.cn

Abstract

We demonstrate a neural machine translation web service. Our NMT service provides web-based translation interfaces for a variety of language pairs. We describe the architecture of NMT runtime pipeline and the training details of NMT models. We also show several applications of our online translation interfaces.

1 Introduction

Neural machine translation (NMT) (Bahdanau et al., 2015; Cho et al., 2014; Sutskever et al., 2014) has achieved great success in recent years and significantly outperforms statistical machine translation on various language pairs (Sennrich et al., 2016a; Wu et al., 2016; Zhou et al., 2016). More and more companies and institutes begin to deploy NMT engines on their machine translation services (Wu et al., 2016; Crego et al., 2016).

We published our NMT online service[1] on November 2016. Up to now, we support nine translation directions: Simplified Chinese ↔ English, Simplified Chinese ↔ Tibetan, Uyghur → Simplified Chinese, Mongolian → Simplified Chinese, Indonesian → Simplified Chinese, Vietnamese → Simplified Chinese, and Deutsch → English. We have also implemented Simplified-Traditional Chinese conversion in the same framework.

In this paper, we describe the implementation and deployment of our NMT online service. Different from (Junczys-Dowmunt et al., 2016) and (Stahlberg et al., 2017), which introduced fast and usable decoding tools, we mainly focus on the NMT runtime pipeline architecture and the details of training NMT models. We introduce a

language-independent NMT service framework, which is capable with different types of neural decoders. We report effective techniques and tricks to optimize the training of NMT models. We also present several applications of using our online service.

2 System Architecture

We implement a language-independent pipeline framework. The pipeline consists of six abstract interfaces: paragraph analyzer, tokenizer, subword segmenter, decoder, detokenizer, and paragraph reconstructor. To deploy a new NMT engine, we only need to implement the corresponding interfaces for the specific language or directly reuse the existing ones.

The **paragraph analyzers** parse the paragraphs into sentences and records the relationship between sentences and paragraphs. We simply implement a rule-based sentence segmenter for each source language.

Tokenizers used in the online runtime must be identical to the one used in the training time. The Moses[2] tokenizers and truecasers are applied on source languages like English and Deutsch and in-home word segmenters are applied on Chinese and Tibetan. For Mongolian and Uyghur, we first tokenize the sentence using our own tokenizer and then latinize and normalize the sentence to reduce the vocabulary.[3] For Simplified-Traditional Chinese conversion, we simply split sentences into characters.

Subword segmenters are effective to reduce the vocabulary and enable the translation of out-

---

[*]Corresponding author.

[1]http://nmt.cloudtrans.org/

[2]http://statmt.org/moses/

[3]The details of our tokenization method, including word segmentation, latinization, and normalization, have been described in our technical reports of WMT17, CWMT2017 and WAT2017 translation tasks (Tan et al., 2017a,b; Wang et al., 2017).

The Companion Volume of the IJCNLP 2017 Proceedings: System Demonstrations, pages 29–32,
Taipei, Taiwan, November 27 – December 1, 2017. ©2017 AFNLP

of-vocabulary tokens. We implement two different types of subword segmenters. For languages with explicit boundaries between syllables, like Chinese and Tibetan, we use mixed word/character model (Wu et al., 2016). We keep a shortlist of the most frequent words and split other words into syllables. Unlike (Wu et al., 2016), we do not add any extra prefixes or suffixes to the segmented syllables. For languages without explicit boundaries between syllables, like English, Deutsch, Mongolian and Uyghur, we use the BPE method[4] (Sennrich et al., 2016c).

Different beam search **decoders** are implemented to support different types of neural models.

- **Translation model**: Our NMT model is a modified version of `dl4mt`[5]. Therefore, we implement a variant of AmuNMT C++ decoder[6] to support our NMT models and achieve parallel decoding.

- **Transliteration model**: We regard Simplified-Traditional Chinese conversion as a sequence labeling task and resort to a simple transliteration model, which is a single layer bi-directional GRU with a softmax layer on the top. In decoding, we employ a Simplified-Traditional Chinese character conversion table to prune the search space.

We apply the Moses **detokenizer** and truecaser on the output English sentences[7]. We use several heuristic rules to judge whether each space in the output Chinese/Tibetan sentences should be kept or not.

The **paragraph reconstructors** use the results of the paragraph analyzers to restore the output paragraphs.

3 Training Details

3.1 Training Data

We crawled monolingual and parallel data from Internet. We filter out bad sentences and utilize target language monolingual data by back-translation method (Sennrich et al., 2016b).

Before training a translation model, we filter out bad sentence pairs from parallel data according to their ratio of length and alignment scores obtained by `fast-align` toolkit[8].

We use `srilm`[9] to train a 5-gram KN language model on the monolingual data of target language and select monolingual sentences according to their perplexity. We train backward translation models on the parallel data and translate the selected monolingual sentences back to the source language.

In our preliminary experiments, we found that training or tuning on the synthetic training data alone could not improve the performance of NMT models. Therefore, we randomly sample a comparable amount of bilingual sentence pairs from parallel data and mix them up with the synthetic ones.

For resource-rich language pairs, such as Chinese-English, we first train a NMT model on the parallel data and then fine-tune the model on the mixed synthetic data. For low-resource language pairs, we found that tuning pre-trained models on mixed synthetic data can not improve the translation quality. Instead, we directly train NMT models on the mixed synthetic data and achieve significant improvement[10].

For Simplified-Traditional Chinese conversion, we utilize our Traditional Chinese corpora[11] to synthesize training data by using our ruled based Traditional-Simplified Chinese converter[12].

3.2 Hyper-parameters

For translation models, we use Adam optimizer (Kingma and Ba, 2015) ($\beta_1 = 0.9$, $\beta_2 = 0.999$ and $\epsilon = 1 \times 10^{-8}$) and set the initial learning rate to 5×10^{-4}. During the training process, we clip the norm of gradient to a predefined value of 5.0 and gradually halve the learning rate. We use dropout (Srivastava et al., 2014) to avoid overfitting with a keep probability of 0.8. For each language pair, we train a variety of NMT models with different data shuffling and random initialization and apply the ensembling method, which is pro-

---

[4] `https://github.com/rsennrich/subword-nmt`

[5] `https://github.com/nyu-dl/dl4mt-tutorial`

[6] `https://github.com/emjotde/amunmt`

[7] The suffixes adding by BPE segmenters plus the followed spaces are removed first.

[8] `https://github.com/clab/fast_align`

[9] `http://www.speech.sri.com/projects/srilm/`

[10] The details of our experiments have been described in our technical reports of WMT17, CWMT2017 and WAT2017 translation tasks (Tan et al., 2017a,b; Wang et al., 2017).

[11] `http://cloudtranslation.cc/corpus_tc.html`

[12] `http://jf.cloudtranslation.cc/`

posed by (Sutskever et al., 2014), to generate better translation.

For transliteration models, the settings are almost the same as above, except that we use the RMSprop optimizer (Tieleman and Hinton, 2012) and do not use dropout and ensemble technique.

4 Applications

Using our free online translation interface[13], developers can easily access to NMT engines. We have developed several applications using the NMT interface:

- **Web Page Translator**: We have published a free web page translation interface[14] using NMT engines. When a client requests an URL, we first crawl the web page and extract the text contents, and then call the NMT interface to get the corresponding translations and replace the source contents.

- **Speech-to-speech Translator**: We have published a free speech-to-speech translation service on WeChat Platform as an official account named *self-talker*. When receiving audio messages from users, we use the speech recognition feature of WeChat Platform to get the recognition results and call our NMT interface to get the translation, then pass into Buidu TTS API[15] to synthesize the speech and response to the user. Currently, we only support Chinese-English translation.

- *Yunyi* **CAT Platform**: *Yunyi* is our computer-aided translation platform. Traditionally, CAT systems use example-based or statistics-based MT engines as their backends. Now, on *Yunyi* platform, we provide human translators with NMT engines to achieve better translations and less efforts of post-editing.

5 Conclusion and Future Works

We presented the architecture and training details of our NMT online service, as well as several applications of using our translation interfaces. Currently, We have completed our main implementation and are in the process of testing new features, including the incremental update of translation models and the support of user-defined translation memories and lexicons. We plan to support more language pairs in the future, especially the low-resource ones, including {Thai, Malay, Hindi} $\leftrightarrow$ Simplified Chinese.

Acknowledgments

This work was supported by the Natural Science Foundation of China (Grant No. 61573294), the Ph.D. Programs Foundation of Ministry of Education of China (Grant No. 20130121110040), the Foundation of the State Language Commission of China (Grant No. WT135-10) and the National High-Tech R&D Program of China (Grant No. 2012BAH14F03).

References

Dzmitry Bahdanau, KyungHyun Cho, and Yoshua Bengio. 2015. Neural machine translation by jointly learning to align and translate. In *Proceedings of ICLR*.

Kyunghyun Cho, Bart van Merrienboer, Caglar Gulcehre, Dzmitry Bahdanau, Fethi Bougares, Holger Schwenk, and Yoshua Bengio. 2014. Learning phrase representations using RNN encoder–decoder for statistical machine translation. In *Proceedings of EMNLP*, pages 1724–1734.

Josep Maria Crego, Jungi Kim, Guillaume Klein, Anabel Rebollo, Kathy Yang, Jean Senellart, Egor Akhanov, Patrice Brunelle, Aurelien Coquard, Yongchao Deng, Satoshi Enoue, Chiyo Geiss, Joshua Johanson, Ardas Khalsa, Raoum Khiari, Byeongil Ko, Catherine Kobus, Jean Lorieux, Leidiana Martins, Dang-Chuan Nguyen, Alexandra Priori, Thomas Riccardi, Natalia Segal, Christophe Servan, Cyril Tiquet, Bo Wang, Jin Yang, Dakun Zhang, Jing Zhou, and Peter Zoldan. 2016. Systrans pure neural machine translation systems. *arXiv preprint arXiv:1610.05540*.

Marcin Junczys-Dowmunt, Tomasz Dwojak, and Hieu Hoang. 2016. Is neural machine translation ready for deployment? A case study on 30 translation directions. In *Proceedings of the 9th International Workshop on Spoken Language Translation (IWSLT)*.

Diederik Kingma and Jimmy Ba. 2015. Adam: A method for stochastic optimization. In *Proceedings of ICLR*.

Rico Sennrich, Barry Haddow, and Alexandra Birch. 2016a. Edinburgh neural machine translation systems for WMT 16. *arXiv preprint arXiv:1606.02891*.

---

[13]`http://nmt.cloudtrans.org/nmt?`
`src=<UrlEncodedSourceText>&lang=`
`<LanguagePairCode>`

[14]`http://nmt.cloudtrans.org/url?`
`url=<UrlEncodedOriginalUrl>&dir=`
`<LanguagePairCode>`

[15]`http://yuyin.baidu.com/`

Rico Sennrich, Barry Haddow, and Alexandra Birch. 2016b. Improving neural machine translation models with monolingual data. In *Proceddings of ACL*, pages 86–96.

Rico Sennrich, Barry Haddow, and Alexandra Birch. 2016c. Neural machine translation of rare words with subword units. In *Proceedings of ACL*, pages 1715–1725.

Nitish Srivastava, Geoffrey Hinton, Alex Krizhevsky, Ilya Sutskever, and Ruslan Salakhutdinov. 2014. Dropout: A simple way to prevent neural networks from overfitting. *The Journal of Machine Learning Research*, 15(1):1929–1958.

Felix Stahlberg, Eva Hasler, Danielle Saunders, and Bill Byrne. 2017. SGNMT – a flexible NMT decoding platform for quick prototyping of new models and search strategies. *arXiv preprint arXiv:1707.06885*.

Ilya Sutskever, Oriol Vinyals, and Quoc V Le. 2014. Sequence to sequence learning with neural networks. In *Advances in neural information processing systems*, pages 3104–3112.

Zhixing Tan, Boli Wang, Jinming Hu, Yidong Chen, and Xiaodong Shi. 2017a. XMU neural machine translation systems for WMT 17. In *Proceedings of the Second Conference on Machine Translation, Volume 2: Shared Task Papers*, pages 400–404.

Zhixing Tan, Boli Wang, Xiansong Ji, Bingyansen Wu, Jinming Hu, Yidong Chen, and Xiaodong Shi. 2017b. XMU neural machine translation systems for CWMT 2017. In *Proceddings of the 13th China Workshop on Machine Translation*.

Tijmen Tieleman and Geoffrey Hinton. 2012. Lecture 6.5-rmsprop: Divide the gradient by a running average of its recent magnitude. *COURSERA: Neural Networks for Machine Learning*.

Boli Wang, Zhixing Tan, Jinming Hu, Yidong Chen, and Xiaodong Shi. 2017. XMU neural machine translation systems for WAT 2017. In *Proceedings of the 4th Workshop on Asian Translation (WAT2017)*.

Yonghui Wu, Mike Schuster, Zhifeng Chen, Quoc V Le, Mohammad Norouzi, Wolfgang Macherey, Maxim Krikun, Yuan Cao, Qin Gao, Klaus Macherey, et al. 2016. Google's neural machine translation system: Bridging the gap between human and machine translation. *arXiv preprint arXiv:1609.08144*.

Jie Zhou, Ying Cao, Xuguang Wang, Peng Li, and Wei Xu. 2016. Deep recurrent models with fast-forward connections for neural machine translation. *Transactions of the Association for Computational Linguistics*, 4:371–383.

Semantics-Enhanced Task-Oriented Dialogue Translation:
A Case Study on Hotel Booking

Longyue Wang[†]   **Jinhua Du**[†]   **Liangyou Li**[§]   **Zhaopeng Tu**[‡*]   **Andy Way**[†]   **Qun Liu**[†]

[†]ADAPT Centre, School of Computing, Dublin City University, Ireland

{longyue.wang, jinhua.du, andy.way, qun.liu}@adaptcentre.ie

[§]Noah's Ark Lab, Huawei Technologies, China   [‡]Tencent AI Lab, China

liliangyou@huawei.com   zptu@@tencent.com

Abstract

We showcase **TODAY**, a semantics-enhanced task-oriented dialogue translation system, whose novelties are: (i) task-oriented named entity (NE) definition and a hybrid strategy for NE recognition and translation; and (ii) a novel grounded semantic method for dialogue understanding and task-order management. TODAY is a case-study demo which can efficiently and accurately assist customers and agents in different languages to reach an agreement in a dialogue for the hotel booking.

1   Introduction

Applications of machine translation (MT) in some human–human communication scenarios still exist many challenging problems due to the characteristics of spoken languages and dialogues. For example, general-purpose MT systems cannot perform efficiently and effectively on specific tasks such as hotel booking because of the low accuracy of entity recognition and translation in dialogues between customers and hotel agents as shown below:

Source:	我想定个房间，{十二月二十五号} (星期二) [三点]入住。
Reference:	I would like to reserve a room on {December the 25th}, (Tuesday) and I will check in at [three o'clock].
Google:	I'd like to have a room, [three] on (Tuesday), {February 25}.
App1:	I want to book a room, (Two) or [Three] rooms at the {December 25} week.

In this example, *App1* is a commercialised translation system for the travel domain. We found that check-in date/time and week day were not translated correctly either by *Google* or *App1*. Wrong

translations of these entities will impede communication between the customer and agent.

We showcase our task-oriented semantics-enhanced dialogue machine translation (DMT) system **TODAY**[1] which alleviates these problems for the hotel booking scenario.

2   System Description

In the hotel booking scenario, customers and agents speak different languages.[2] Customers access the hotel website to request a conversation, and the agent accepts the customer's request to start the conversion. Figure 1 shows the detailed workflow of TODAY. We first recognise entities by inferring their specific types based on information such as contexts, speakers etc. (cf. Section 2.1 and 2.2). Then, the recognised entities will be represented as logical expressions or semantic templates using the grounded semantics module (cf. Section 2.2). Finally, candidate translations of semantically represented entities will be marked up and fed into a unified bi-directional translation process.

2.1   Task-Oriented Named Entity Recognition and Translation

As standard types of entities (e.g. people, organizations, locations) cannot exactly match our task-oriented entity types, we define a series of task-oriented entity types in TODAY, including {*time, number, date, currency, room type, person name, hotel name, location, payment type*}. We combine rule-based and dictionary-based methods for our NE recognition and translation. For bilingual dictionary construction, we employ the ICE toolkit.[3] ICE can guide users through a series of linguis-

---

* Work was done when Zhaopeng Tu was working at Huawei Noah's Ark Lab.

[1]The demo system can be found at http://computing.dcu.ie/~lwang/demo.html.

[2]The rest of the paper will assume that customers speak English and agents speak Chinese.

[3]Available at http://nlp.cs.nyu.edu/ice.

The Companion Volume of the IJCNLP 2017 Proceedings: System Demonstrations, pages 33–36,
Taipei, Taiwan, November 27 – December 1, 2017. ©2017 AFNLP

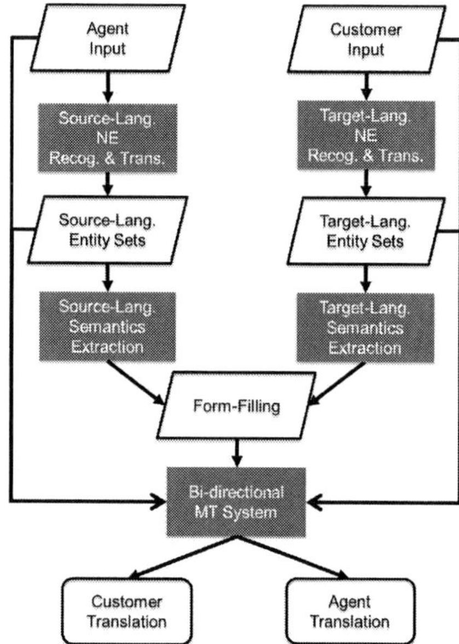

Figure 1: Workflow of TODAY.

Type	Feature	Example value
Customer	Name	John
	Tel. NO.	1234567
Room	Check-In Date	1st April 2017
	Check-Out Date	2nd April 2017
	Room Type	Single
	Price Per. Night	300 Dollars
	Payment Type	VISA
	Card NO.	987654321

Table 1: An example of a booking order which represents the grounded semantic of a dialogue.

tic processing steps, presents them with entities and dependency relations that are potential seeds, and helps them to expand the seeds by answering yes/no questions. Other types of NEs such as time, data etc. can be recognised and translated using rules because of their formulaic and common expressions.

Our hybrid strategy can generates multiple translation candidates. For example, the date have various formats in both English and Chinese. Then the recognised entities and their candidate translations are formalise by XML markup in the source-side sentence. Finally the sentence is fed into the decoder to compete with the translation model.

2.2 Grounded Semantic Representation and Form Filling

We propose a specific semantic module for our task-oriented dialogues: *grounded semantics* module which is in the form of *Feature-Value* (FV) pairs.

In TODAY, we define two types of features (Table 1): customer features and room features. While the customer features include information about the customer of the current order, room features describe the details of the order, including check-in and check-out date, room type, room price, and payment information. All these features and their values can be recognised by the NE recogniser (cf. Section 2.1) but extended by adding extra patterns. These new patterns are used to label an entity with

more detailed categories, such as determining a date to be one of the two features: *check-in date* and *check-out date*. To achieve this, patterns take contexts into consideration. For example, according to the phrase *from 1st Jan to 2nd Jan, 1st Jan* is a check-in date while *2nd Jan* is a check-out date.

After recognising all features and their values, we need to solve conflicts when a feature appears multiple times with different values.

Customer:	I'd like to have a **single** room.
Hotel:	Sorry. I only have **double** rooms available.
Customer:	OK. A **double** room would also be fine.

In this example, the feature *room type* appears three times with values *single* and *double*. To determine which value should be chosen, we propose to score each candidate value of a feature by comparing its contexts with predefined attributes of the feature. The candidate with the highest score is then taken as the final feature value.

We define four attributes on each feature:

- *Speaker*: Its value is either *hotel* or *customer*. For example, because the room type is usually chosen by a customer, we define the speaker attribute of this feature to be "customer".

- *Position*: It defines a range of positions in dialogues that a feature should be within. For example, we define the position attribute of a customer name as [1–3], because a dialogue usually starts from self-introduction and greetings, but in other features we set the position to infinity.

- $Pattern_{cur}$: It consists of a set of patterns that usually appear in the current utterance. For example, the customer name usually follows *I am* or *my name is*.

- $Pattern_{pre}$: It consists of a set of patterns that usually appear in the previous utterance.

Given these predefined attributes on a feature, we calculate a score for each candidate value of the feature, according to Equation (1):

$$Score(v) = S \cdot P \cdot (\lambda_c + M_c) \cdot (\lambda_p + M_p) \quad (1)$$

where $S \in \{0, 1\}$ indicates whether the current speaker equals to the speaker defined in the feature or not, $P \in \{0, 1\}$ denotes whether the position of the feature is within the range given by its position attributes or not, and M_c and M_p are the number of matched patterns in the current utterance and previous utterance, respectively. We use $\lambda_c = 1$ and $\lambda_p = 1$ as smooth factors.

3 Experiments and Analysis

3.1 Setup

From the IWSLT DIALOG corpus, we select 1,023 and 1053 hotel booking sentences (34/36 dialogues) as development set and test set, respectively. We combine our home-made travel domain corpora as in-domain training data (180K). We also use domain adaptation techniques to select in-domain data from movie subtitles (Wang et al., 2016b).

We carry out our experiments using the phrase-based SMT model in Moses (Koehn et al., 2007) on Chinese (ZH)–English (EN). Furthermore, we train a 5-gram language model using the SRI Language Toolkit (Stolcke, 2002). We run GIZA++ (Och and Ney, 2003) for alignment and use MERT (Och, 2003) to optimize the feature weights. We develop TODAY on the basis of an open-source live support application Mibew[4] by integrating our semantics-enhanced SMT system and the semantic form filling.

3.2 Evaluation of Dialogue Translation

We first evaluate the domain adaptation and NE approaches on DMT, respectively. Then, we combine these best sub-models to further improve the translation quality.

The baseline systems are trained on the in-domain corpus and the results show that an MT system trained on small-scale data can only obtain 24.20 and 17.90 BLEU points on English–Chinese and Chinese–English, respectively. Combining the models trained on the selected pseudo in-domain data can improve the performance by at most +1.09 and +1.24 on EN-ZH (top-50K) and ZH-EN (top-50K), respectively. However, bring more pseudo in-domain data ($> top - 250K$), the performance drops sharply.

---

[4]Available at `https://mibew.org`.

System	EN-ZH	△	ZH-EN	△
In-domain	24.20	-	17.90	-
1-best Entity	30.70	+6.5	20.30	+2.4
N-best Entity	31.10	+6.9	20.20	+2.3

Table 2: Performance with task-oriented NE recognition.

Task	SYS	BLEU (%)
ZH-EN	Google	10.3
	App1	10.4
	TODAY	21.5
EN-ZH	Google	16.9
	App1	15.5
	TODAY	32.7

Table 3: Overall performance.

About NE component, we employ XML markup technique to insert bilingual entities into the translation. As the entity may have multiple translations, we also explore N-best entity lists. After inserting entities into the MT system, the performance improves by +6.5 (EN-ZH) and +2.4 (ZH-EN) BLEU points as shown in Table 2. When using the N-best entity method, it can further improve the performance by +0.4 BLEU on English–Chinese.

Based on the individual performance of each component, we design our DMT: 1) build translation models on selected top-50K data and combine it with baseline; 2) integrate N-best NE models to our MT our system. In Table 3, it shows that combination further improve the translation performance. Comparing with App1 and Google Translate, our system significantly outperforms these systems by +17.2 and +11.2 BLEU points on EN-ZH and ZH-EN, respectively.

3.3 Evaluation of Task-Oriented Named Entity and Translation

We manually annotated Chinese and English sentences in the test set to evaluate the proposed task-oriented NE recognition and translation in terms of accuracy, recall and F1. In Table 4, **Recog** indicates NE recognition on the source language, and **Trans** indicates translation task. All F1 scores are over 90% in terms of recognition and translation,

Lang	Task	Acc. (%)	Rec. (%)	F1 (%)
ZH-EN	Recog	98.21	99.76	98.99
	Trans	91.86	93.33	92.59
EN-ZH	Recog	97.78	96.04	96.90
	Trans	97.24	95.52	96.37

Table 4: Results of NE recognition and translation.

Task	SYS	Trans. Acc. (%)
ZH-EN	Google	72.08
	App1	85.28
	TODAY	97.24
EN-ZH	Google	58.11
	App1	66.42
	TODAY	95.52

Table 5: Comparison on entity translation with different systems.

Feature	Precision (%)
Customer Name	97.1
Customer Tel. NO.	91.2
Check-In Date	100.0
Check-Out Date	76.5
Room Type	73.5
Price Per. Night	79.4
Payment Type	100.0
Card NO.	97.1
Average	89.4

Table 6: Performance of form-filling (EN).

which shows that the proposed fine-grained NE definitions and hybrid strategy for NE recognition and translation is effective in TODAY.

We also compared TODAY with Google and App1 as shown in Table 5. Since we cannot obtain NE recognition information from both third-part applications, we manually inspected the top-300 sentences (in test set) and only calculate accuracy of translations of entities. If the translation of an entity matches the reference, we count it as correct; otherwise, it is regarded as incorrect. It shows that TODAY significantly outperforms both Google and App1 in terms of accuracy of entity translation.

3.4 Evaluation of Grounded Semantic Extraction

We tested our grounded semantic module on the test set in terms of feature recognition and form filling. Each dialogue is manually annotated with semantic features and has an associated order form as a reference. Since our feature recognizer is a simple extension of the NE recogniser, in this section we ignore the performance of the recognizer. Table 6 shows evaluation results of the form-filling given golden feature annotations.

Five features (*customer name, customer Tel. NO., check-in date, payment type*, and *Card NO.*) achieve an accuracy over 90%. The reason of such high accuracy we analyse is that there are fewer conflicts for them in a single dialogue. By contrast, on the other 3 features, (*check-out date, room type*, and *price per. night*) the accuracy is between 70%–80%. By inspecting the dialogues, we found that (i) the *check-out date* is not always explicitly mentioned in the dialogues; (ii) the *room type* and *price per. night* have a relatively higher repetition. These observations suggest that it is harder to solve the conflicts on these three features.

4 Conclusion and Future Work

In this paper we described TODAY, a semantics-enhanced task-oriented dialogue translation system for hotel booking scenarios and evaluated its performance. In future work, we plan to integrate neural MT into our demo system based on our advanced approaches (Wang et al., 2016a, 2017).

Acknowledgments

This work is supported by the Science Foundation of Ireland (SFI) ADAPT project (Grant No.:13/RC/2106), and partly supported by the DCU-Huawei Joint Project (Grant No.:201504032-A (DCU), YB2015090061 (Huawei)).

References

Philipp Koehn, Hieu Hoang, Alexandra Birch, Chris Callison-Burch, Marcello Federico, Nicola Bertoldi, Brooke Cowan, and et al. 2007. Moses: Open source toolkit for statistical machine translation. In *Proceedings of the 45th ACL: Demo and Poster Sessions*, pages 177–180.

Franz Josef Och. 2003. Minimum error rate training in statistical machine translation. In *Proceedings of the 41st ACL*, pages 160–167.

Franz Josef Och and Hermann Ney. 2003. A systematic comparison of various statistical alignment models. *Computational Linguistics*, 29(1):19–51.

Andreas Stolcke. 2002. SRILM – an extensible language modeling toolkit. In *Proceedings of the 7th ICSLP*, pages 901–904.

Longyue Wang, Zhaopeng Tu, Andy Way, and Qun Liu. 2017. Exploiting cross-sentence context for neural machine translation. In *Proceedings of the 2017 EMNLP*, pages 2816–2821.

Longyue Wang, Zhaopeng Tu, Xiaojun Zhang, Hang Li, Andy Way, and Qun Liu. 2016a. A novel approach for dropped pronoun translation. In *Proceedings of the 2016 NAACL*, pages 983–993.

Longyue Wang, Xiaojun Zhang, Zhaopeng Tu, Andy Way, and Qun Liu. 2016b. The automatic construction of discourse corpus for dialogue translation. In *Proceedings of the 10th LREC*, pages 2748–2754.

NNVLP: A Neural Network-Based Vietnamese Language Processing Toolkit

Thai-Hoang Pham
Alt Inc
Hanoi, Vietnam
phamthaihoang.hn@gmail.com

Xuan-Khoai Pham
FPT University
Hanoi, Vietnam
khoaipxmse0060@fpt.edu.vn

Tuan-Anh Nguyen
Alt Inc
Hanoi, Vietnam
ntanh.hus@gmail.com

Phuong Le-Hong
Vietnam National University
Hanoi, Vietnam
phuonglh@vnu.edu.vn

Abstract

This paper demonstrates neural network-based toolkit namely NNVLP for essential Vietnamese language processing tasks including part-of-speech (POS) tagging, chunking, named entity recognition (NER). Our toolkit is a combination of bidirectional Long Short-Term Memory (Bi-LSTM), Convolutional Neural Network (CNN), Conditional Random Field (CRF), using pre-trained word embeddings as input, which achieves state-of-the-art results on these three tasks. We provide both API and web demo[1] for this toolkit.

1 Introduction

Vietnamese belongs to the top 20 most spoken languages and is employed by an important community all over the world. Therefore, research on Vietnamese language processing is an essential task. This paper focuses on three main tasks for Vietnamese language processing including POS tagging, chunking, and NER.

In this paper, we present a state-of-the-art system namely NNVLP for the Vietnamese language processing. NNVLP toolkit outperforms most previously published toolkits on three tasks including POS tagging, chunking, and NER. The contributions of this work consist of:

- We demonstrate a neural network-based system reaching the state-of-the-art performance for Vietnamese language processing including POS tagging, chunking, and NER. Our

system is a combination of Bi-LSTM, CNN, and CRF models, which achieves an accuracy of 91.92%, F_1 scores of 84.11% and 92.91% for POS tagging, chunking, and NER tasks respectively.

- We provide our API and web demo for user, which is believed to positively contributing to the long-term advancement of Vietnamese language processing.

The remainder of this paper is structured as follows. Section 2 summarizes related work on Vietnamese language processing. Section 3 describes NNVLP toolkit architecture, API, and web interface. Section 4 gives experimental results and discussions. Finally, Section 5 concludes the paper.

2 Related Works

Previously published systems for Vietnamese language processing used traditional machine learning methods such as Conditional Random Field (CRF), Maximum Entropy Markov Model (MEMM), and Support Vector Machine (SVM). In particular, most of the toolkits for POS tagging task attempted to use conventional models such as CRF (Tran and Le, 2013) and MEMM (Le-Hong et al., 2010). (Tran and Le, 2013) also used CRF for chunking task. Recently, at the VLSP 2016 workshop for NER task, several participated system use MEMM (Le-Hong, 2016), (Nguyen et al., 2016) and CRF (Le et al., 2016) to solve this problem.

3 NNVLP API and Web Demo

3.1 System Architecture

We implement the deep neural network model described in (Pham and Le-Hong, 2017a). This

---

[1]nnvlp.org

The Companion Volume of the IJCNLP 2017 Proceedings: System Demonstrations, pages 37–40,
Taipei, Taiwan, November 27 – December 1, 2017. ©2017 AFNLP

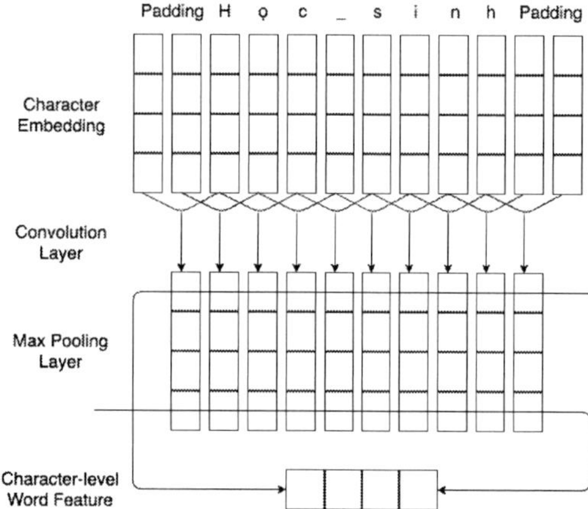

Figure 1: The CNN layer for extracting character-level word features of word *Học_sinh* (Student).

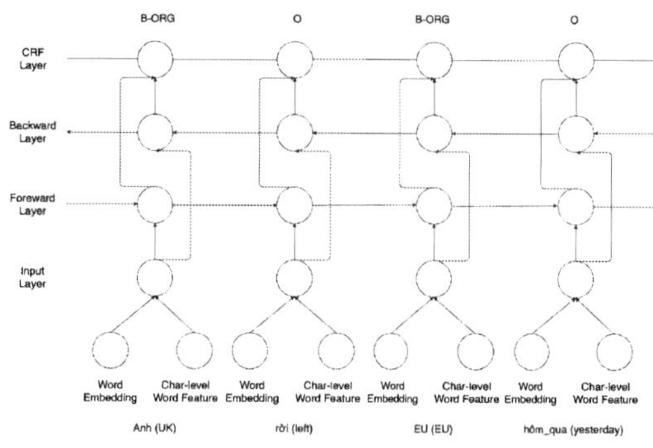

Figure 2: The Bi-LSTM-CRF layers for input sentence *Anh rời EU hôm qua.* (UK left EU yesterday.)

model is a combination of Bi-directional Long Short-Term Memory (Bi-LSTM), Convolutional Neural Network (CNN), and Conditional Random Field (CRF). In particular, this model takes as input a sequence of the concatenation of word embedding pre-trained by word2vec[2] tool and character-level word feature trained by CNN. That sequence is then passed to a Bi-LSTM, and then a CRF layer takes as input the output of the Bi-LSTM to predict the best named entity output sequence. Figure 1 and Figure 2 describe the architectures of BI-LSTM-CRF layers, and CNN layer respectively.

NNVLP toolkit uses these architectures for all tasks including POS tagging, chunking, and NER. Because each word in the Vietnamese language

may consist of more than one syllables with spaces in between, which could be regarded as multiple words by the unsupervised models, we, first, segment the input texts into sequences of words by pyvi toolkit[3]. These word sequences are put into NNVLP toolkit to get corresponding POS tag sequences. Next, these words and POS tag sequences are put into NNVLP toolkit to get corresponding chunk sequences. Finally, NNVLP toolkit takes as input sequences of the concatenation of word, POS tag, and chunk to predict corresponding NER sequences. Figure 3 presents this pipeline of NNVLP toolkit.

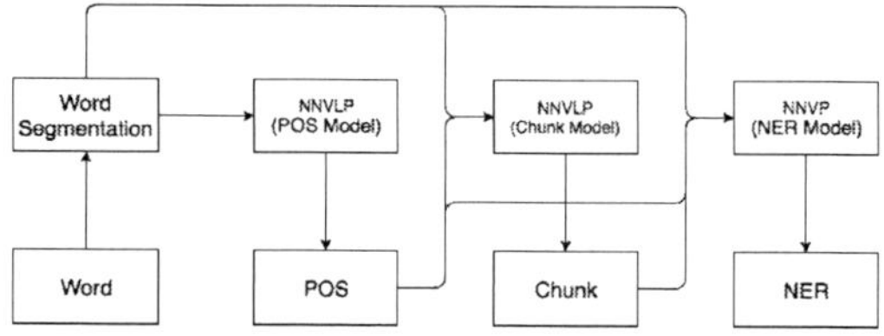

Figure 3: The Architecture of NNVLP Toolkit

3.2 NNVLP API

NNVLP API is an API for Vietnamese Language Processing which takes input sentences and outputs a JSON containing a list of sentences where each word in these sentences has POS tag, chunk, named entity attributes as shown in Figure 4.

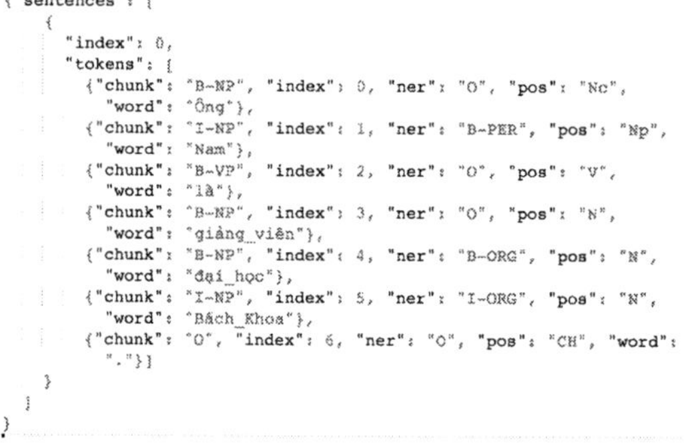

{"sentences": [
    {
      "index": 0,
      "tokens": [
        {"chunk": "B-NP", "index": 0, "ner": "O", "pos": "Nc",
          "word": "Ông"},
        {"chunk": "I-NP", "index": 1, "ner": "B-PER", "pos": "Np",
          "word": "Nam"},
        {"chunk": "B-VP", "index": 2, "ner": "O", "pos": "V",
          "word": "là"},
        {"chunk": "B-NP", "index": 3, "ner": "O", "pos": "N",
          "word": "giảng_viên"},
        {"chunk": "B-NP", "index": 4, "ner": "B-ORG", "pos": "N",
          "word": "đại_học"},
        {"chunk": "I-NP", "index": 5, "ner": "I-ORG", "pos": "N",
          "word": "Bách_Khoa"},
        {"chunk": "O", "index": 6, "ner": "O", "pos": "CH", "word":
          "."}]
    }
  ]
}

Figure 4: The output JSON of the input sentence "Ông Nam là giảng viên đại học Bách Khoa." (Mr Nam is a lecturer of Bach Khoa University.)

[2]https://code.google.com/archive/p/word2vec/

[3]https://pypi.python.org/pypi/pyvi

3.3 Web Demo

We also provide web interface[4] for users of NNVLP toolkit. Users can type or paste raw texts into the textbox and click *Submit* button to get the corressponding POS tag, chunk, named entity sequences. Each label is tagged with different color to make the output easy to see. Users can also look up the meaning of each label by click *Help* button. Figure 5 presents the web interface of our system.

4 Experiments

In this section, we compare the performance of NNVLP toolkit with other published toolkits for Vietnamese including Vitk (Le-Hong et al., 2010), vTools (Tran and Le, 2013), RDRPOSTagger (Nguyen et al., 2014), and vie-ner-lstm (Pham and Le-Hong, 2017b).

4.1 Data Sets

To compare fairly, we train and evaluate these systems on the VLSP corpora. In particular, we conduct experiments on Viet Treebank corpus for POS tagging and chunking tasks, and on VLSP shared task 2016 corpus for NER task. All of these corpora are converted to CoNLL format. The corpus of POS tagging task consists of two columns namely word, and POS tag. For chunking task, there are three columns namely word, POS tag, and chunk in the corpus. The corpus of NER task consists of four columns. The order of these columns are word, POS tag, chunk, and named entity. While NER corpus has been separated into training and testing parts, the POS tagging and chunking data sets are not previously divided. For this reason, we use 80% of these data sets as a training set, and the remaining as a testing set. Because our system adopts early stopping method, we use 10% of these data sets from the training set as a development set when training NNVLP system. Table 1 and Table 2[5] shows the statistics of each corpus.

4.2 Evaluation Methods

We use the accuracy score that is the percentage of correct labels to evaluate the performance of each system for POS tagging task. For chunking and NER tasks, the performance is measured with F_1 score, where $F_1 = \frac{2*P*R}{P+R}$. Precision (P) is the

---

[4]nnvlp.org

[5]For more details about these tagsets, please visit the demo website at nnvlp.org

	Number of sentences		
Data sets	POS	Chunk	NER
Train	7268	7283	14861
Dev	1038	1040	2000
Test	2077	2081	2831

Table 1: The number of sentences for each part in POS tagging, chunking, and NER data sets

Data sets	Labels
POS	N, V, CH, R, E, A, P, Np, M, C, Nc, L, T, Ny, Nu, X, B, S, I, Y, Vy
Chunk	NP, VP, PP, AP, QP, RP
NER	PER, LOC, ORG, MISC

Table 2: Labels in POS tagging, chunking, and NER data sets

percentage of chunks or named entities found by the learning system that are correct. Recall (R) is the percentage of chunks or named entities present in the corpus that are found by the system. A chunk or named entity is correct only if it is an exact match of the corresponding phrase in the data file.

4.3 Experiment Results

We evaluate performances of our system and several published systems on POS tagging, chunking, and NER data sets. Inputs for POS tagging task are words, for chunking task are words and POS tags, and for NER task are words, POS tags, and chunks. Table 3, Table 5, and Table 6 present the performance of each system on POS tagging, chunking, and NER task respectively. The hyper-parameters for training NNVLP are given in Table 4.

System	Accuracy
Vitk	88.41
vTools	90.73
RDRPOSTagger	91.96
NNVLP	**91.92**

Table 3: Performance of each system on POS tagging task

By combining Bi-directional Long Short-Term Memory, Convolutional Neural Network, and Conditional Random Field, our system outperforms most published systems on these three tasks. In particular, NNVLP toolkit achieves an accuracy of 91.92%, F_1 scores of 84.11% and 92.91% for

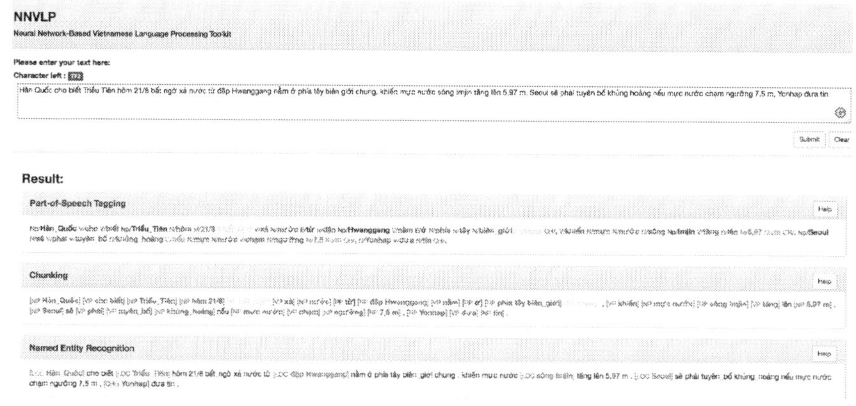

Figure 5: The Web Interface of NNVLP Toolkit

Layer	Hyper-parameter	Value
CNN	window size	3
	number of filters	30
LSTM	hidden nodes	300
Embedding	word	300
	character-level	30

Table 4: Hyper-parameters of our models

System	P	R	F1
vTools	82.79	83.55	83.17
NNVLP	83.93	84.28	**84.11**

Table 5: Performance of each system on chunking task

System	P	R	F1
Vitk	88.36	89.20	88.78
vie-ner-lstm	91.09	93.03	92.05
NNVLP	92.76	93.07	**92.91**

Table 6: Performance of each system on NER task

POS tagging, chunking, and NER tasks respectively.

5 Conclusion

We present a neural network-based toolkit for Vietnamese processing that is a combination of Bi-LSTM, CNN, and CRF. The system takes raw sentences as input and produces POS tag, chunk and named entity annotations for these sentences. The experimental results showed that NNVLP toolkit achieves state-of-the-art results on three tasks including POS tagging, chunking, and NER.

References

Thanh Huong Le, Thi Thu Trang Nguyen, Trong Huy Do, and Xuan Tung Nguyen. 2016. Named entity recognition in Vietnamese text. In *Proceedings of VLSP*, Hanoi, Vietnam.

Phuong Le-Hong. 2016. Vietnamese named entity recognition using token regular expressions and bidirectional inference. In *Proceedings of VLSP*, Hanoi, Vietnam.

Phuong Le-Hong, Azim Roussanaly, Thi Minh Huyen Nguyen, and Mathias Rossignol. 2010. An empirical study of maximum entropy approach for part-of-speech tagging of Vietnamese texts. In *TALN*, pages 50–61, Montreal, Canada.

Dat Quoc Nguyen, Dai Quoc Nguyen, Dang Duc Pham, and Son Bao Pham. 2014. RDRPOSTagger: A Ripple Down Rules-based Part-Of-Speech Tagger. In *Proceedings of the Demonstrations at EACL*, pages 17–20, Gothenburg, Sweden.

Thi Cam Van Nguyen, Thai Son Pham, Thi Hong Vuong, Ngoc Vu Nguyen, and Mai Vu Tran. 2016. Dsktlab-ner: Nested named entity recognition in Vietnamese text. In *Proceedings VLSP*, Hanoi, Vietnam.

Thai-Hoang Pham and Phuong Le-Hong. 2017a. End-to-end recurrent neural network models for Vietnamese named entity recognition: Word-level vs. character-level. In *Proceedings of PACLING*, pages 251–264, Yangon, Myanmar.

Thai-Hoang Pham and Phuong Le-Hong. 2017b. The importance of automatic syntactic features in Vietnamese named entity recognition. In *Proceedings of PACLIC*, Cebu, Philippines.

Mai-Vu Tran and Duc-Trong Le. 2013. vTools: Chunker and part-of-speech tools. *RIVF-VLSP 2013 Workshop*.

ClassifierGuesser: A Context-based Classifier Prediction System for Chinese Language Learners

Nicole Peinelt[1,2] and **Maria Liakata**[1,2] and **Shu-Kai Hsieh**[3]

[1]The Alan Turing Institute, London, UK
[2]Department of Computer Science, University of Warwick, Coventry, UK
[3]Graduate Institute of Linguistics, National Taiwan University, Taipei, Taiwan
{n.peinelt, m.liakata}@warwick.ac.uk, shukaihsieh@ntu.edu.tw

Abstract

Classifiers are function words that are used to express quantities in Chinese and are especially difficult for language learners. In contrast to previous studies, we argue that the choice of classifiers is highly contextual and train context-aware machine learning models based on a novel publicly available dataset, outperforming previous baselines. We further present use cases for our database and models in an interactive demo system.

1 Introduction

Languages such as Chinese are characterized by the existence of a class of words commonly referred to as 'classifiers' or 'measure words'. Based on syntactic criteria, classifiers are the obligatory component of a quantifier phrase which is contained in a noun phrase or verb phrase.[1] Semantically, a classifier modifies the quantity or frequency of its head word and requires a certain degree of shared properties between classifier and head. Although native speakers select classifiers intuitively, language learners often struggle with the correct usage of classifiers due to the lack of a similar word class in their native language. Moreover, no dictionary or finite set of rules covers all possible classifier-head combinations exhaustively.

Previous research has focused on associations between classifiers and nominal head words in isolation and included approaches based on ontologies (Mok et al., 2012; Morgado da Costa et al., 2016), databases with semantic features of Chinese classifiers (Gao,

2011), as well as an SVM with syntactic and ontological features (Guo and Zhong, 2005). However, without any context classifier assignment can be ambiguous. For instance, the noun 球 'ball' can be modified by *ke* - a classifier for round objects - when referring to the object itself as in (1), but requires the event classifier *chang* in the context of a ball match as in (2). We argue that context is an important factor for classifier selection, since a head word may have multiple associated classifiers, but the final classifier selection is restricted by the context.

(1) 一 颗 红色 的 球
one *ke* red DE ball
'a red ball'

(2) 一 场 精彩 的 球
one *chang* exciting DE ball
'an exciting match'

This study introduces a large-scale dataset of everyday Chinese classifier usage for machine learning experiments. We present a model that outperforms previous frequency and ontology baselines for classifier prediction without the need for extensive linguistic preprocessing and head word identification. We further demonstrate the usefulness of the database and our models in use cases.

2 System Design

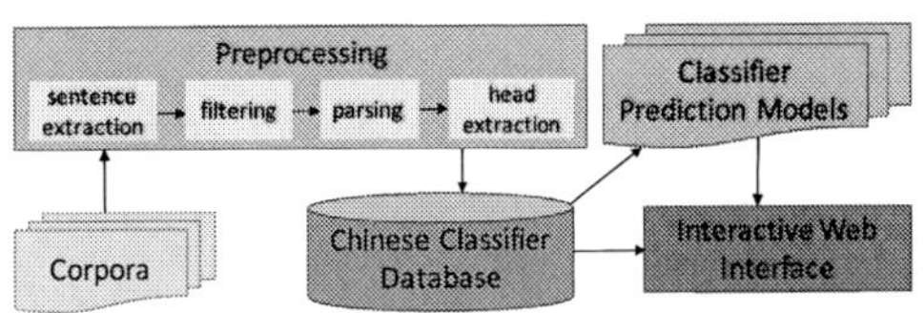

Figure 1: Overview of proposed system

---

[1]Following Huang (1998) and 何杰 (2008) we include verbal as well as nominal classifiers.

The Companion Volume of the IJCNLP 2017 Proceedings: System Demonstrations, pages 41–44,
Taipei, Taiwan, November 27 – December 1, 2017. ©2017 AFNLP

Figure 1 gives an overview of our system. It comprises data collection, pre-processing and the compilation of the Chinese Classifier Database (section 2.1), the training of classifier prediction models (section 2.2), and the interactive online interface (section 3).

2.1 The Chinese Classifier Database

The database is based on three openly available POS tagged Chinese language corpora: The Lancaster Corpus of Mandarin Chinese (McEnery and Xiao, 2004), the UCLA Corpus of Written Chinese (Tao and Xiao, 2012) and the Leiden Weibo Corpus (van Esch, 2012). Sentences from the corpora were assigned unique ids, filtered for the occurrence of classifier POS tags and cleaned in a number of filtering steps in order to improve the data quality (Table 1). We further parsed the remaining sentences with the Stanford constituent parser (Levy and Manning, 2003) and extracted the head of the classifier in each sentence based on the parse tree.[2] By manually evaluating 100 randomly sampled sentences from the database, we estimate a classifier identification accuracy of 91% and head identification accuracy of 78%. Based on our observations, most errors are due to accumulating tokenisation, tagging and parsing errors, as well as elliptic classifier usage. In addition to the example sentences, we also included lexical information from CC-Cedict[3] for the 176 unique classifier types.

Applied filters	Sentences	%
None (initial corpus)	2,258,003	100
1. duplicate sentence	1,553,430	69
2. <4 or >60 tokens in sentence	1,470,946	65
3. classifiers consisting of letters/numbers; or <70% of Chinese material in sentence	1,437,491	64
4. tagged classifiers are in fact measure units (e.g. 毫米)	1,150,749	51
5. classifiers with <10 examples	1,109,871	49
6. classifier fails manual check	1,103,338	49
7. frequent error patterns	1,083,135	48
8. multiple classifiers in a single sentence	858,472	38

Table 1: Number of remaining sentences in database. Matching sentences are excluded.

2.2 Classifier Prediction

2.2.1 Task

Following the only previous machine learning approach (Guo and Zhong, 2005), we frame classifier prediction as a multi-class classification problem. However, in contrast to previous work that focused on word-based classifier prediction, we adapt the prediction task for a sentence-based scenario, which is a more natural and less ambiguous task than predicting classifiers without context. Not all sentences in the Chinese classifier database contain head words, due to co-referential and anaphoric usage. Hence, we query the database for sentences in which both the head word and corresponding classifier were identified, resulting in 681,102 sentences. This subset is randomly split into training (50%), development (25%) and test set (25%). In each sentence with an identified classifier and corresponding head word, we substitute the classifier with the gap token <CL> and use the classifier as its class label. For example, the tagged sentence

我们是一 <c> 家 </c> <h> 人 </h>。

is transformed into the training example

我们是一 <CL> <h> 人 </h>。

with the label '家'. Labels are simplified from tokens to types by reducing duplicate classifiers (e.g. 个个 → 个) and mapping traditional characters to simplified characters (e.g. 個 → 个), resulting in a dataset[4] with 172 distinct classes.[5] Given a training set of observed sentences and classifiers, the task is to fill the gap in a sentence with the most appropriate classifier.

2.2.2 Baseline approaches

As previous studies have evaluated algorithms on individually collected unpublished data, we implement the following baselines to compare our models with previous results:

- *ge*: always assign the universal and most common noun classifier 个 (Guo and Zhong, 2005; Morgado da Costa et al., 2016).

---

[2]Starting from the position of the classifier, we move one node up in the tree at a time until reaching a noun or verb phrase and extract its head word.

[3]https://cc-cedict.org/

[4]We make our dataset publicly available at https://github.com/wuningxi/ChineseClassifierDataset.

[5]The number of unique classifiers differs from the full database because only example sentences with identified head words are taken into account.

- *pairs*: assign the classifier most frequently observed in combination with this head word during training; assign 个 for unseen words (Guo and Zhong, 2005).

- *concepts*: assign classifiers based on classifier-concept pair counts using the Chinese Open Wordnet and 个 for unseen words (Morgado da Costa et al., 2016).

2.2.3 Context-based models

Previous approaches predominantly rely on ontological resources, which require a lot of human effort to build and maintain, resulting in limited coverage for new words and domains. We use distributed representations to capture word similarity based on syntactic behaviour, as they can be trained unsupervised on a large scale and are easily adapted on new language material. We train word embeddings with word2vec (Mikolov et al., 2013) on sentences from the original three corpora and also obtain pre-trained word embeddings from Bojanowski et al. (2017). The pre-trained embeddings consistently achieve better results and are hence used in all subsequent experiments.

Since the head word is linguistically the most important factor for classifier selection, we first train two widely used machine learning models (SVM, Logistic Regression) on the embedding vector of the head word (*head*). In order to investigate to which extend context may help with classifier prediction, we then gradually add more contextual features to the models: With the motivation of reducing head word ambiguity, we include embedding vectors of words within window size $n=2$ of the head word ($cont_h$). Furthermore, we add embedding vectors of words surrounding the classifier gap ($cont_{cl}$) to capture the typical immediate environment of different classifiers. As

preliminary experiments indicate that increasing the window size to $n>2$ increases computation costs without significant performance gains, a better approach to include more context is needed. We hence use a bidirectional LSTM (Hochreiter and Schmidhuber, 1997) to encode the entire sentence excluding any head word annotation ($cont_{cl}$) and predict classifiers based on the last hidden state (Figure 2).

2.2.4 Results

We report micro F1 (accuracy) and macro F1 scores for each model after hyper-parameter tuning in Table 3. The head-classifier combination baseline gives a strong result, which the SVM and Logistic Regression models trained on only headword embedding vectors cannot surpass. Global corpus statistics on classifiers outperform the local information captured by the word embeddings in this case. Adding head word context features successfully reduces the ambiguity of head words and results in a significant improvement over the baseline. Including contextual features of the classifier gap slightly decreases the performance, but still outperforms the context-unaware models. The best model is the LSTM which achieves micro F1 71.51 and macro F1 30.56 on the test set based on the full sentence context without the need for headword identification (hyper-parameters as reported in Table 2, optimiser: Adam, learning rate: 0.001).

Parameter	Values
Hidden units	160, 224, 320, 384, **480**
Dropout rate	**0.0**, 0.25, 0.5
Batch size	32, **64**, 96, 128

Table 2: Tuned hyper-parameters for LSTM. Terms in bold represent final settings.

	Features	Micro F1		Macro F1	
		dev	test	dev	test
base line	ge	45.12	45.21	0.36	0.37
	pairs	61.82	61.72	24.40	23.80
	concepts	49.08	49.11	8.40	7.94
svm	head	53.67	53.72	13.33	13.56
	+$cont_h$	66.02	66.02	24.86	24.39
	+$cont_{cl}$	58.97	58.83	22.23	21.75
log reg	head	57.61	57.72	15.99	15.66
	+$cont_h$	67.81	67.67	28.95	27.37
	+$cont_{cl}$	67.43	67.29	27.51	26.70
lstm	$cont_s$	**71.69**	**71.51**	**31.56**	**30.56**

Table 3: Model performance on the classifier prediction task (logreg = Logistic Regression).

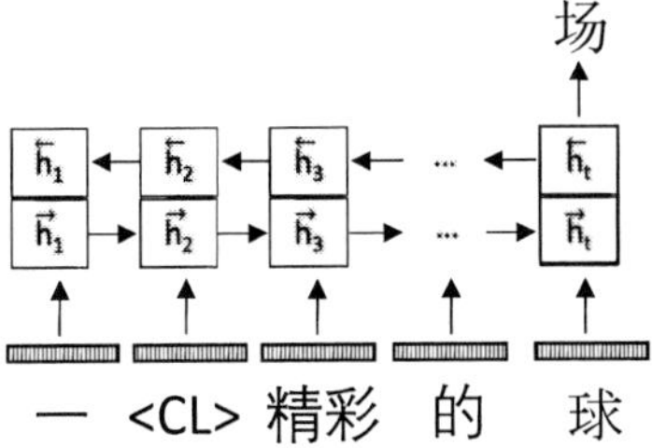

Figure 2: LSTM architecture for context-based classifier prediction.

3   Use Cases

When learning new classifiers, Chinese language learners can obtain frequency statistics from the online interface of the Chinese Classifier Database [6] to focus on the most commonly used and most important classifiers. Learners can explore a visualisation of frequently used classifier-head word combinations in an interactive bar plot (Figure 3, left) which displays example sentences from the database when clicking on the bars. Furthermore, the ClassifierGuesser (Figure 3, right) can be used when learners want to compose a sentence but don't know the appropriate classifier. After inputing a sentence with a gap, the system predicts the best classifier candidate based on the *pairs* baseline and the best LSTM model.

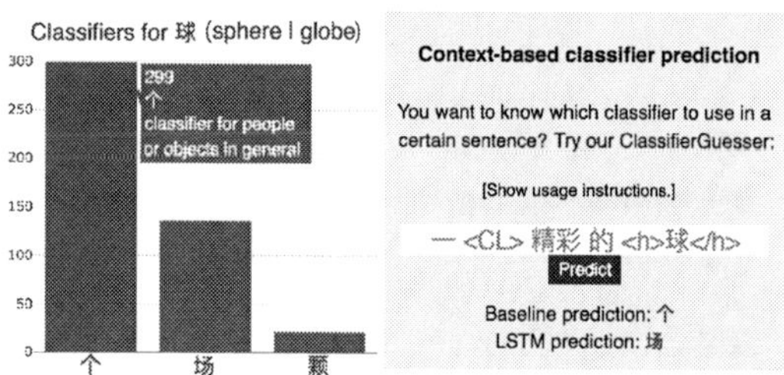

Figure 3: Screenshot of classifier-head pair visualisation (left) and ClassifierGuesser (right).

4   Conclusion

This paper introduced a system for predicting Chinese classifiers in a sentence. Based on a novel dataset of example sentences for authentic usage of Chinese classifiers, we conducted multiple machine learning experiments and found that incorporating context improves Chinese classifier prediction over word-based models. Our best model clearly outperforms the baselines and does not require manual feature engineering or extensive preprocessing. We argue that including contextual features can help resolve ambiguities and context-based classifier prediction is a more realistic task than isolated head word-based prediction. We further presented an interactive web system to access our database and pre-trained models and demonstrated possible use cases for language learners.

---

[6]chinese-classifier-database.azurewebsites.net

Acknowledgments

This work was supported by The Alan Turing Institute under the EPSRC grant EP/N510129/1, Microsoft Azure and the German Academic Exchange Service (DAAD).

References

Piotr Bojanowski, Edouard Grave, Armand Joulin, and Tomas Mikolov. 2017. Enriching Word Vectors with Subword Information. *Transactions of the Association for Computational Linguistics*, 5:135–146.

Helena Hong Gao. 2011. E-learning design for Chinese classifiers: Reclassification. *Communications in Computer and Information Science*, 177:186–199.

Hui Guo and Huayan Zhong. 2005. Chinese classifier assignment using SVMs.

Sepp Hochreiter and Jürgen Schmidhuber. 1997. Long short-term memory. *Neural computation*, 9(8):1735–1780.

C.-T. James Huang. 1998. *Logical relations in Chinese and the theory of grammar*. Taylor & Francis, New York & London.

Roger Levy and Christopher Manning. 2003. Is it harder to parse chinese, or the chinese treebank? In *Proceedings of the 41st Annual Meeting on ACL-Volume 1*, pages 439–446.

Anthony McEnery and Zhonghua Xiao. 2004. The Lancaster Corpus of Mandarin Chinese: A corpus for monolingual and contrastive language study.

Tomas Mikolov, Kai Chen, Greg Corrado, and Jeffrey Dean. 2013. Efficient estimation of word representations in vector space. *arXiv preprint arXiv:1301.3781*.

Hazel Mok, Shu Wen, Gao Huini Eshley, and Francis Bond. 2012. Using WordNet to predict numeral classifiers in Chinese and Japanese. In *GWC 2012 6th International Global Wordnet Conference*, pages 264–271.

Luis Morgado da Costa, Francis Bond, and Helena Gao. 2016. Mapping and Generating Classifiers using an Open Chinese Ontology. In *Proceedings of the 8th Global WordNet Conference*, pages 247–254.

Hongyin Tao and Richard Xiao. 2012. *The UCLA Chinese Corpus (2nd edition)*. UCREL.

Daan van Esch. 2012. Leiden Weibo Corpus. http://lwc.daanvanesch.nl/.

何杰. 2008. 现代汉语量词研究: 增编版. 北京语言大学出版社, 北京市.

Automatic Difficulty Assessment for Chinese Texts

John Lee, Meichun Liu, Chun Yin Lam, Tak On Lau, Bing Li, Keying Li
Department of Linguistics and Translation
City University of Hong Kong
jsylee@cityu.edu.hk, meichliu@cityu.edu.hk, mickey1224@gmail.com,
tolau2@cityu.edu.hk, bli232-c@my.cityu.edu.hk, keyingli3-c@my.cityu.edu.hk

Abstract

We present a web-based interface that automatically assesses reading difficulty of Chinese texts. The system performs word segmentation, part-of-speech tagging and dependency parsing on the input text, and then determines the difficulty levels of the vocabulary items and grammatical constructions in the text. Furthermore, the system highlights the words and phrases that must be simplified or re-written in order to conform to the user-specified target difficulty level. Evaluation results show that the system accurately identifies the vocabulary level of 89.9% of the words, and detects grammar points at 0.79 precision and 0.83 recall.

1 Introduction

Reading is critical to foreign language acquisition (Krashen, 2005). While language textbooks provide a convenient source of reading materials, these materials are limited in quantity and do not always match the language learners' interest. To supplement textbooks, teachers often utilize texts from other sources, such as newspapers, magazines and the web. Since they were not originally written for pedagogical purposes, these texts typically require adjustments: teachers must simplify or re-write difficult vocabulary items and grammatical constructions so that the text becomes "comprehensible input" (Krashen and Mason, 2015) to the learners; conversely, teachers might desire more advanced language usage to challenge the learners. This editing process can be time consuming and labor intensive.

To assist the editor, we built a web-based interface that automatically determines the difficulty level of Chinese texts. It detects vocabulary items

and grammar points covered by the *Hanyu Shuiping Kaoshi* (HSK) guidelines, the official curriculum for Chinese as a foreign language (CFL) in mainland China. Furthermore, the editor can specify a target difficulty level, and ask the interface to highlight all words and grammatical constructions that must be simplified or re-written to reach the target level.

To the best of our knowledge, this is the first system that assists editors of CFL pedagogical material by explicitly pinpointing the words and grammatical constructions that exceed the target difficulty level in an official curriculum.

2 Previous Work

Most text difficulty assessment systems aim at native speakers, both for Chinese (Chen et al., 2013; Sung et al., 2015) and for other languages (Pitler and Nenkova, 2008; Sato et al., 2008). Among those that target language learners, most give a holistic score on the overall difficulty level of the text (François and Fairon, 2012; Pilán et al., 2014), but do not specifically indicate the difficult words or grammatical constructions. Hence, while these systems can help identify suitable reading material for language learners (Brown and Eskenazi, 2004), they are not designed to facilitate editing of language teaching materials, which is the goal of our system.

Targeting learners of English as a foreign language, *FLAIR* (Chinkina et al., 2016) can detect 87 linguistic forms in the official English curriculum in a German state. The system attains an average precision and recall of 0.94 and 0.90 in detecting grammar points. Most systems for CFL determine the difficulty level of a text on the basis of vocabulary difficulty alone. ChineseTA (Chu, 2005), for example, estimate vocabulary difficulty on the basis of word frequencies interpolated from var-

The Companion Volume of the IJCNLP 2017 Proceedings: System Demonstrations, pages 45–48,
Taipei, Taiwan, November 27 – December 1, 2017. ©2017 AFNLP

Sentence	据说， *jushuo* 'reportedly'	齐白石 *qibaishi* 'Qibaishi'	一开始 *yikaishi* 'at first'	画 *hua* 'paint'	的 *de* DE	虾 *xia* 'shrimp'	太 *tai* too	重 *zhong* 'emphasize'	写真 *xiezhen* 'realism'
	"It is said that realism was overly emphasized in the shrimps painted by Qibaishi in early times."								
Vocabulary	5	NR	6+	3	1	6+	1	5	6+
Grammar	5 Parenthetical expression	3 Relative clause with subject and predicate		-	-		1 Adverb of degree	1 Verbal predicate	

Table 1: Vocabulary and grammar difficulty level of an example sentence, according to the HSK scale. "NR" refers to a proper noun; 6+ is the vocabulary level attributed to words not found in the HSK vocabulary lists.

Lv	Vocab. items	Gram. points	Lv	Vocab. items	Gram. points
1	150	35	4	1200	38
2	150	58	5	2500	39
3	600	68	6	5000	28

Table 2: Number of vocabulary items and grammar points at each HSK level

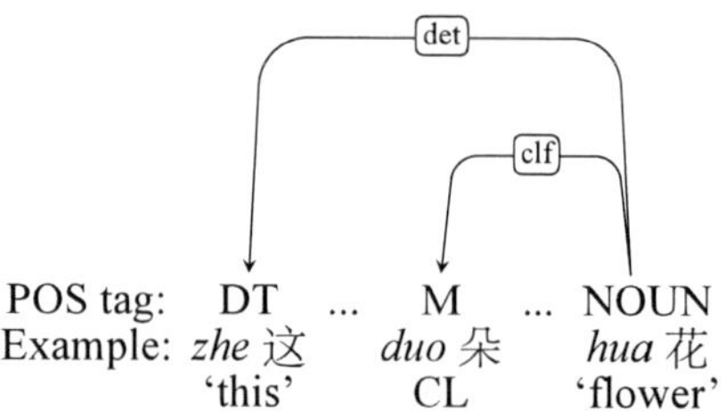

Figure 1: Parse tree pattern, in Stanford Dependencies for Chinese, for detecting the grammar point "Determiner and classifier"

ious corpora. The *Guidelines for CLT Materials Development* website (http://www.cltguides.com), the system that is most similar to ours, also concentrates on vocabulary assessment. It can detect a number of grammar constructions, but does not indicate their HSK levels or specific grammar points.

3   System Description

For Chinese as a foreign language, the two major assessment scales are the *Test of Chinese as a Foreign Language* (Zeng, 2014) and the *Hanyu Shuiping Kaoshi* (HSK) (Hanban, 2014). Both contain six levels and can be mapped to the Common European Framework of Reference for Languages, a global standard for measuring foreign language proficiency. Our system adopts HSK, the more widely used of the two in mainland China.

Upon input of any Chinese passage, the system performs word segmentation, POS tagging and dependency parsing using the Stanford Parser (Manning et al., 2014). It then offers difficulty assessment in terms of vocabulary and grammar (Section 3.1), and guides the user in editing the sentence towards the target difficulty level (Section 3.2).

3.1   Difficulty assessment

The HSK guidelines provide a vocabulary list and a set of grammar points for each level; as shown in Table 2), there are a total of 9,600 vocabulary items and 266 grammar points. For vocabulary assessment, the system matches each word with these lists, but does not assess the difficulty level of proper nouns, except those included in the HSK scheme. Table 1 shows an example sentence; the vocabulary difficulty levels of its word range from level 1 (e.g., *tai* 'too') to 6+ (e.g., *xiezhen* 'realism'); *Qibaishi*, a proper name, is not assigned any level.

For grammar assessment, we manually crafted parse tree patterns for the grammar points. A pattern may contain a combination of constraints in lexical, POS and dependency features. Figure 1 shows the pattern for the grammar point "Determiner and classifier" (指示代词和量词), requiring a noun to have two modifiers in the 'det' and 'clf' relations. The system performs dependency parsing on the input text, and then searches for matching parse tree patterns. In Table 1, the sentence exhibits four grammar points, the highest of which is the use of "Parenthetical expression" (*jushuo*, 'reportedly'), at level 5.

Most grammar points in the HSK guidelines provide concrete examples. The only exception is the grammar point for quadrasyllabic idiomatic expressions (成語), for which we use a list of about 1,000 expressions collected from Wiktionary. Further, three grammar points — semantic passive (意

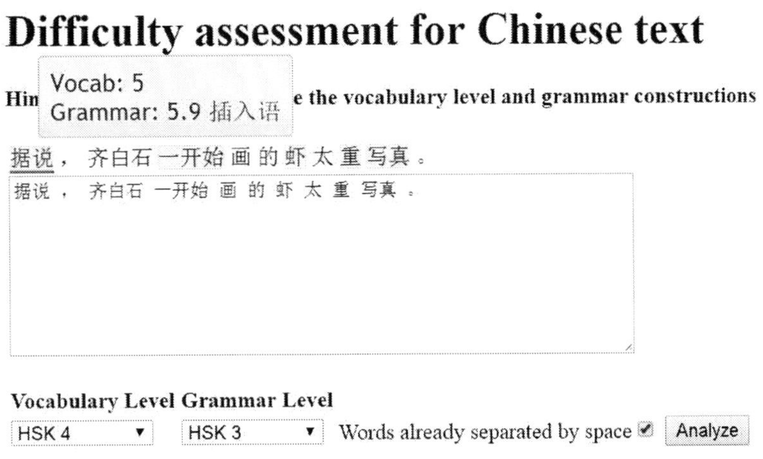

Figure 2: Screenshot of the system on input of the Chinese sentence in Table 1, with level 4 as the target vocabulary level, and level 3 as the target grammar level. The interface (i) highlights in yellow all words (*jushuo* 'reportedly', *yikaishi* 'at first', *xia* 'shrimp', *zhong* 'emphasize', and *xiezhen* 'realism') that exceed level 4; and (ii) underlines in red all grammatical points (*jushuo*) that exceed level 3.

义上的被动词), rhetorical questions with interrogative pronouns (用疑问代词的反问句) and directional complement (趋向补语) — require deeper semantic analysis, and thus have not been implemented.

3.2 Editing

If the user specifies the target vocabulary level and grammar level, the interface highlights in yellow all words that exceed the target level, and underlines in red all words participating in grammar structures that exceed the target level. For detailed information, the user can mouse over each word to view the vocabulary level detected, as well as the name of the grammatical structure detected (Figure 2). The user can edit the text accordingly, then re-submit the updated version for assessment, in an iterative manner until the text reaches the desired level of difficulty, or when the percentage of words exceeding the level falls below an accepted threshold, as shown by the distribution of statistics at the bottom of the page.

In case the system's word segmentation is inaccurate, the user may correct it and re-submit the text with the option "Words already separated by space", thereby asking the system to adopt the manual segmentation.

Level	# sentences	# words	# grammar points
1	18	105	69
2	51	407	296
3	52	639	403
4	60	1241	540
5	65	1211	577
6	85	1970	801

Table 3: Statistics of the evaluation dataset

4 Evaluation

In order to evaluate system performance, we harvested sentences from sample HSK exams from levels 1 to 6, obtained from the chinesetest.cn website. Our dataset contained a total of 331 sentences, including all sentences in the "Reading" sections of the examination papers for levels 1 to 4, and all sentences from reading comprehension exercises for levels 5 and 6. We performed manual word segmentation on these sentences, and annotated the HSK levels of each individual word and grammatical construction; Table 3 shows statistics of this dataset.

We evaluated system performance on both vocabulary and grammar assessment on this dataset; Table 4 presents the results according to HSK level. For vocabulary assessment, using automatic word segmentation, the system correctly recog-

Level	Vocabulary	Grammar	
	Accuracy	Precision	Recall
1	0.810	0.747	0.812
2	0.958	0.962	0.865
3	0.890	0.960	0.896
4	0.895	0.649	0.778
5	0.898	0.739	0.842
6	0.891	0.670	0.777

Table 4: System accuracy on vocabulary assessment, and precision and recall on grammar point detection

nized overall 89.9% of words and their vocabulary level. Most errors are due to word segmentation errors during automatic parsing, or misrecognition of proper names.

The average precision and recall of grammar points are 0.788 and 0.828. The system performs best in categories involving lexical features with unambiguous POS, such as "Pronouns" (人称代词), and worse in categories that requires accurate dependency parsing, such as double object (双宾语). Errors in recall were mostly due to the non-exhaustive nature of the examples in the HSK guidelines. Precision is most challenging for grammar points that can be disambiguated only through semantic analysis, for example between the use of *hui* (会) to express ability vs. prediction.

5 Conclusions and future work

We have presented a web-based interface that automatically assesses the difficulty level of a Chinese text. The system indicates the vocabulary level and grammar level of specific words and grammatical structures according to the HSK scale, and highlight those that need to be simplified or re-written in order for the text to conform to the target level. We have also reported the performance of the system on vocabulary and grammar level assessment.

In future work, we plan to estimate the overall difficulty level of a sentence; to offer suggestions for lexical simplification; and to extend the scope to other linguistic features, beyond the HSK guidelines, that can help estimate the difficulty of a text.

References

Jonathan Brown and Maxine Eskenazi. 2004. Retrieval of authentic documents for reader-specific lexical practice. In *Proc. InSTIL/ICALL Symposium*. Venice, Italy.

Yu-Ta Chen, Yaw-Huei Chen, and Yu-Chih Cheng. 2013. Assessing chinese readability using term frequency and lexical chain. *Computational Linguistics and Chinese Language Processing* 18(2):1–18.

Maria Chinkina, Madeeswaran Kannan, and Detmar Meurers. 2016. Online Information Retrieval for Language Learning. In *Proc. ACL System Demonstrations*.

Chengzhi Chu. 2005. ChineseTA 1.1. Beijing Language and Culture University Press, Beijing, China.

Thomas François and Cédric Fairon. 2012. An "AI Readability" Formula for French as a Foreign Language. In *Proc. EMNLP-CONLL*.

Hanban. 2014. *International Curriculum for Chinese Language and Education*. Beijing Language and Culture University Press, Beijing, China.

S. Krashen. 2005. Free voluntary reading: New research, applications, and controversies. In G. Poediosoedarmo, editor, *Innovative approaches to reading and writing instruction, Anthology Series 46*. SEAMEO Regional Language Centre, Singapore, pages 1–9.

S. Krashen and B. M. Mason. 2015. Can Second Language Acquirers Reach High Levels of Proficiency through Self-selected Reading? *International Journal of Foreign Language Teaching* 10(2):10–19.

Christopher D. Manning, Mihai Surdeanu, John Bauer, Jenny Finkel, Steven J. Bethard, and David McClosky. 2014. The Stanford CoreNLP Natural Language Processing Toolkit. In *Proc. ACL System Demonstrations*. pages 55–60.

Ildikó Pilán, Elena Volodina, and Richard Johansson. 2014. Rule-based and Machine Learning Approaches for Second Language Sentence-level Readability. In *Proc. 9th Workshop on Innovative Use of NLP for Building Educational Applications*.

Emily Pitler and Ani Nenkova. 2008. Revisiting readability: a unified framework for predicting text quality. In *Proc. EMNLP*.

Satoshi Sato, Suguru Matsuyoshi, and Yohsuke Kondoh. 2008. Automatic Assessment of Japanese Text Readability based on a Textbook Corpus. In *Proc. LREC*.

Yao-Ting Sung, Ju-Ling Chen, Ji-Her Cha, Hou-Chiang Tseng, Tao-Hsing Chang, and Kuo-En Chang. 2015. Constructing and validating readability models: the method of integrating multilevel linguistic features with machine learning. *Behavior Research Methods* 47:340–354.

Wenxuan Zeng. 2014. Huayu baqianci ciliang fenji yanjiu 华语八千词词汇分级研究 (Classification on Chinese 8 000 Vocabulary). *Huayu xuekan* 华语学刊 6:22–33.

Verb Replacer: An English Verb Error Correction System

Yu-Hsuan Wu[1], Jhih-Jie Chen[2], Jason S. Chang[1]
[1]Institute of Information Systems and Applications
National Tsing Hua University
[2] Department of Computer Science
National Tsing Hua University
{shanny, jjc, jason}@nlplab.cc

Abstract

According to the analysis of Cambridge Learner Corpus, using a wrong verb is the most common type of grammatical errors. This paper describes *Verb Replacer*, a system for detecting and correcting potential verb errors in a given sentence. In our approach, alternative verbs are considered to replace the verb based on an error-annotated corpus and verb-object collocations. The method involves applying regression on channel models, parsing the sentence, identifying the verbs, retrieving a small set of alternative verbs, and evaluating each alternative. Our method combines and improves channel and language models, resulting in high recall of detecting and correcting verb misuse.

1 Introduction

It is estimated that over 1 billion people are learning English around the world, 600 to 700 million of which are English as a second language (ESL). Lacking lexical and collocation knowledge, ESL learners often have difficulties in choosing an appropriate word to fit the context.

Consider a learner's sentence "All Japanese children *accept* a solid education.". For most non-native English writers, this sentence may seem like an acceptable sentence. However, the verb *accept* is not appropriate and *receive* would be a better choice. Many learners misuse *accept* when they should use *receive* because these two verbs are semantically similar and have the same translation in learners native language. Therefore, it is difficult for learners to choose from the two to fit the context (i.e., the object *education*), leading to an awkward sentence.

According to the analysis of a sample of the Cambridge Learner Corpus (CLC) with 1,244 exam scripts for First Certificate English (FCE), verb selection errors (Replace-Verb errors, RV) is the most common error type, not counting spelling errors. In content word (e.g., verb and noun) errors correction, previous systems relied on mostly manually constructed resources (e,g., (Shei and Pain, 2000; Lee and Seneff, 2008; Liu et al., 2009)). It is not clear whether these manual resources can be easily scaled up and extended to other types of writing error and domains. Classifiers have been used for correcting verb errors. (Wu et al., 2010) describe an approach based on a classifier to predict the verb in the context of a given sentence. The main difference from our current work is that in(Wu et al., 2010), the context alone determine the outcome, the channel model information related to the potentially wrong verb is not used. Similarly, (Rozovskaya et al., 2014) use classifiers with the notion of verb finiteness to identify certain types of verb errors. (Rozovskaya et al., 2014) only address the agreement, tense, and form verb errors related to a small candidate set, while we deal with the verb selection problem with an open candidate set. In a noisy-channel approach closer to our work, (Sawai et al., 2013) use large learner corpus to construct candidate sets. They show that an GEC system that uses learner corpus outperforms systems that use WordNet and roundtrip translations, improving the performance of verb error detection and suggestion.

In this paper, we present a system, *Verb Replacer*, that uses both learner and web-scale corpora to extract errors to estimate the parameters in a channel model. Our system exploits the regularity of learner errors and a web-scale data set with a goal of maximizing the probability of an GEC system in returning alternatives for correcting misused verbs. An example *Verb Replacer* feedback

The Companion Volume of the IJCNLP 2017 Proceedings: System Demonstrations, pages 49–52,
Taipei, Taiwan, November 27 – December 1, 2017. ©2017 AFNLP

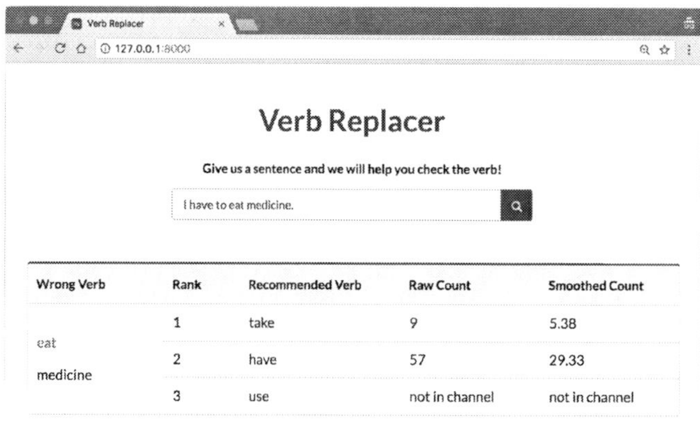

Figure 1: An example *Verb Replacer* search for input "I have to *eat* medicine."

for the sentence "I have to *eat* medicine." is shown in Figure 1.

The rest of this paper is organized as follows. We present our method for obtaining the verb alternatives, re-rank the alternatives and giving the correct suggestions in the next section. We introduce the data and discuss the experimental results in Section 3, and conclude with a summary and future work in Section 4.

2 Methodology

To correct verb misuse in a given sentence, a promising approach is to estimate quantitatively how words are typically misused based on a probabilistic channel model. In this section, we present our method for detecting and correcting RV errors.

2.1 Applying Regression Model

We use the regression model to deal with the data sparseness problem and to smooth the low counts of the channel model. To estimate the parameters of a channel model, we use an correction-annotated corpus to extract instances of Replace-Verb wrong-right pairs. However, some of these verb pairs have low counts, forcing the system to remove candidates with the same count and rank. Thus, we apply a regression model to smooth the low counts. We use Support Vector Regression (SVR) to train the regression model. The features used in the model are shown in Table 1. These features are based on the relationships between the wrong verb and each candidate verb.

There are five types of feature, including thesaurus-based similarity between the wrong

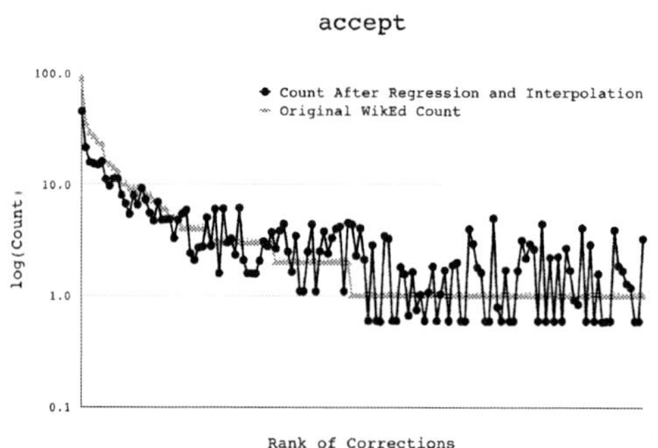

Figure 2: The log(count) before and after regression of a wrong verb *"accept"* to the rank of its corrections

verb and a candidate verb is calculated using a bilingual version of WordNet. We also use conjunction relation refer to the relationship related on the conjunctions *and* and *or* that link the wrong verb and the candidate verb. For a wrong verb X and a candidate verb Y, we first extract ngram with the patterns X *and* Y, X *or* Y, Y *and* X and Y *or* X from Google Web 1T Ngrams Corpus with the counts. Then we check whether both *and* and *or* link X and Y. Additionally, we use the proportion of these two types of patterns as features. Another information source for feature we use is translation. We use bilingual (English to Mandarin) data to find the translation of the wrong verb and a candidate verb, and count the number of translations they shared.

Once we have a regression model, we interpolate the new count with the original count, and a new estimate of count is given to each correction.

Feature	Description
Similarity	WordNet similarity between the wrong verb and a candidate verb
Conjunction relation	AND/OR relation between the wrong verb and a candidate verb
AND Proportion	Proportion of X and Y in all the patterns extracted through AND/OR relation
OR Proportion	Proportion of X or Y in all the patterns extracted through AND/OR relation
Translation	Number of the common words the wrong verb and a candidate verb share in Mandarin translation

Table 1: Features for regression model

Figure 2 shows an example of a wrong verb *accept* from an annotated reference corpus with the count and the rank of its corrections, before and after regression and interpolation.

2.2 Detecting and Correcting RV Errors

We attempt to build a candidate list based on a channel model and collocation list, which is then used to correct RV errors by reranking.

For the error-annotations in each sentence, if the error tag is RV, we keep the misuse verb. Otherwise, we remove the misuses and keep the correction in the sentence. After the sentences are replaced, we assign each token a POS tag. Tokens tagged as VERB are considered as potential errors in the next stage. For simplicity, we do not include auxiliary verbs such as *can*, *will* or *should*.

2.2.1 Building Candidate List

In this stage, we build a candidate list from a channel model and a collocation list. We rank the corrections in the channel model according to their new estimated counts. In order to improve the coverage, we use Google Web1T n-gram data to generate collocations for additional candidate verbs. If a Verb-Obj relation exists in a given learner sentence, the object will be extracted and used to find all of the verbs that are collocated with it. We then reorder the list based on sum of two reciprocal ranks.

2.2.2 Detecting RV Errors

In this stage, we evaluate each verb in the candidate list and rerank them based on a language model. First, the potentially wrong verb in the given sentence is replaced in turn by each verb in the candidate list. Then, the replaced sentences are evaluated based on a language model. We use two trigram language models, trained on a corrected learner corpus and a reference native corpus using SRILM ((Stolcke et al., 2002)), separately. We order the verb in the candidate list according to the log probability provided by the language model. We set a threshold t, and if the original verb ranks

lower than t, the sentence will be returned in the next stage.

2.2.3 Reranking Alternatives

In the final stage, we rerank the alternatives, and suggest appropriate verbs to be returned to learner. For each verb in candidate list, we sum up the score from candidate list itself and the score from language model. Then we rerank the alternatives to suggest top 3 verbs to the user.

3 Experiments and Results

In this section, we describe the training data, development data, and test data we use for the experiments, and introduce the evaluation metrics we use for evaluating the performance of our system. We also show the experimental results.

3.1 Dataset

Wiked Error Corpus (WEC): WEC is a corpus of corrective Wikipedia revision logs. We used these revision edits for estimating the channel model. In total, 480,243 RV wrong-right pairs are extracted from WEC.

The EF-Cambridge Open Language Database (EFCAMDAT): The EFCAMDAT is an English L2 database, we used it for estimating the channel model. These essays were written by English learners, while WEC is composed by native and nonnative domain experts. We obtained around 113,000 RV errors from the dataset.

CLC-FCE Dataset: CLC-FCE Dataset is a collection of essays written by English language learners from around the world. Potential errors have been tagged with the CLC error coding scheme with corrections. We use CLC-FCE for developing and testing. We extracted 3,580 Replace-Verb (RV) errors for test.

3.2 Results for RV Error Detection

Figure 3 shows the results of RV error detection produced by the EFCAM-REG system at threshold t, varying t. If a given sentence with the original verb rank lower than t, the sentence will be handled in the correction step. As we can see in Figure 3, the higher the threshold is set, the higher precision the system can achieve. At threshold 5, the system has the highest F1 score.

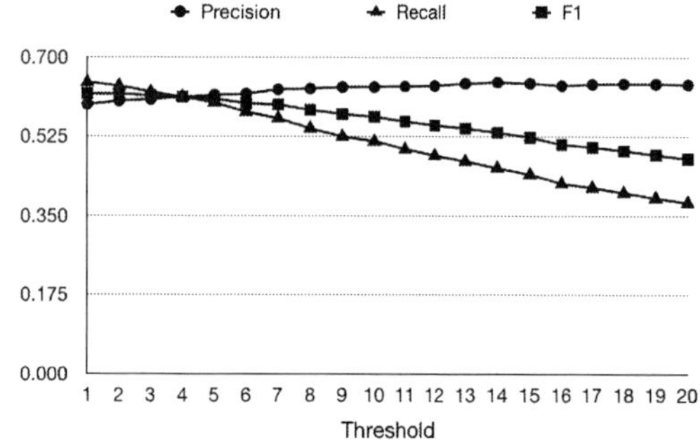

Figure 3: Precision, Recall and F1 score for RV error detection by the EFCAM-REG system at threshold t

3.3 Results for Verb Suggestion

To evaluate performance of suggestion for all erroneous verbs, we use Mean Reciprocal Rank (MRR). In our case, the measure is used to evaluate the Top 3 returned verbs for a given sentence. The MRR is the average of the reciprocal ranks of results for a set of sentences S:

$$MRR = \frac{1}{|S|} \sum_{i=1}^{|S|} \frac{1}{rank_i} \qquad (1)$$

where $rank_i$ refers to the rank position of the gold standard for the $i - th$ sentence.

The results are shown in Table 2. We compare the systems that using WEC and EFCAM-DAT channel model estimating. The results show that the systems with a regression-based channel model (**WEC-REG** and **EFCAM-REG**) perform better than those without regression (**WEC** and **EFCAM**). It is interesting to note that for the top 3 suggestions, using a learner corpus for the channel model estimation plus channel model regression (**EFCAM-REG**) performs the best. Also note that **EFCAM-REG** with the language model trained on the corrected part of EFCAMDAT (**EFCAM-REG-EFLM**) performs the best in terms of offering good suggestions.

4 Conclusion

In summary, we have introduced a new method for detecting and correcting Replace-Verb errors in a given learner sentence based on wrong-right verb pairs in annotated corpora. The analysis shows that our method, combining channel and language models, perform better than without using channel models. The results also show that using a learner corpus for RV error correction achieve better performance than using native reference corpus.

Many avenues exist for future research and improvement of the proposed method. For example, an interesting direction to explore is to use error-annotated sentences to train a sequence to sequence neural network to predict an replace RV errors as well as other types of errors.

Table 2: MRR for verb suggestion over 1,300 sentences

Systems	MRR_3	MRR_{found}
WEC	0.181	0.336
WEC-REG	0.191	0.342
WEC-REG-EFLM	0.190	0.346
EFCAM	0.260	0.428
EFCAM-REG	**0.273**	0.432
EFCAM-REG-EFLM	0.271	**0.446**

References

John Lee and Stephanie Seneff. 2008. Correcting misuse of verb forms. In *Proceedings of ACL-08: HLT*, pages 174–182.

Anne Li-E Liu, David Wible, and Nai-Lung Tsao. 2009. Automated suggestions for miscollocations. In *Proceedings of the 4th Workshop on Innovative Use of NLP for Building Educational Applications*, pages 47–50.

Alla Rozovskaya, Dan Roth, and Vivek Srikumar. 2014. Correcting grammatical verb errors. In *Proceedings of the 14th EACL*, pages 358–367.

Yu Sawai, Mamoru Komachi, and Yuji Matsumoto. 2013. A learner corpus-based approach to verb suggestion for ESL. In *Proceedings of the 51st ACL*, pages 708–713.

C-C Shei and Helen Pain. 2000. An ESL writer's collocational aid. *Computer Assisted Language Learning*, 13(2):167–182.

Andreas Stolcke et al. 2002. Srilm-an extensible language modeling toolkit. In *Interspeech*, volume 2002, page 2002.

Jian-Cheng Wu, Yu-Chia Chang, Teruko Mitamura, and Jason S Chang. 2010. Automatic collocation suggestion in academic writing. In *Proceedings of the 48th ACL*, pages 115–119.

Learning Synchronous Grammar Patterns for Assisted Writing for Second Language Learners

Chi-En Wu, Jhih-Jie Chen, Jim Chang, Jason S. Chang
Department of Computer Science
National Tsing Hua University
{tony, jjc, jim, jason}@nlplab.cc

Abstract

In this paper, we present a method for extracting Synchronous Grammar Patterns (SGPs) from a given parallel corpus in order to assisted second language learners in writing. A grammar pattern consists of a head word (verb, noun, or adjective) and its syntactic environment. A synchronous grammar pattern describes a grammar pattern in the target language (e.g., English) and its counterpart in an other language (e.g., Mandarin), serving the purpose of native language support. Our method involves identifying the grammar patterns in the target language, aligning these patterns with the target language patterns, and finally filtering valid SGPs. The extracted SGPs with examples are then used to develop a prototype writing assistant system, called *WriteAhead/bilingual*. Evaluation on a set of randomly selected SGPs shows that our system provides satisfactory writing suggestions for English as a Second Language (ESL) learners.

1 Introduction

Lexicography is the discipline of analyzing the syntax, semantics, and pragmatics of the language to compile a dictionary, with a description of vocabulary and grammar. The compiling process involves time-consuming delineating word senses, analyzing grammatical information, and providing example sentences. Since 1970s, computational approach of statistical analysis of large-scale corpora was widely adopted in lexicography, which originates from the COBUILD project, led by John Sinclair, aiming at building a large-scale electronic corpus. The COBUILD project lead to dictionaries and grammar books, including *Collins*

COBUILD Grammar Patterns 1: Verbs (Patterns, 1996) and *Collins COBUILD Grammar Patterns 2: Nouns and Adjectives* (Patterns, 1998). These two books describe grammar patterns of common verbs, nouns and adjectives in English, with the concept that most English words tend to follow only a limited set of patterns, which relates to the structure, usage, and the meaning of a word.

Later, Hunston and Francis (2000) propose *Pattern Grammar* with rules describing the intricate relation between word and grammar in one simple representational scheme, which explores the local regularities such as complementation structure, consisting of a headword with a sequence of preposition, noun phrase, verb phrase, clause (e.g., *apologize for n*), or a limited set of special words and phrases.

In this paper, we describe a method for automatically identifying the Chinese counterpart (e.g., "與 n 接觸") of a given English grammar pattern (e.g., "contact with n"), along with the bilingual examples. Such pair of extracted patterns is call a Synchronous Grammar Pattern (SGP). SGPs can be used to support the compilation process of bilingual dictionary reducing the construction time and to improve the learning efficiency of ESL learners. With this in mind, we develop a prototype system, *WriteAway*, to assist writing for Chinese EFL learners.

2 Translation Pattern Assistant

We have implemented a prototype system as a web application, aimed at assisting second language learner in writing with native language support. At run time, *WriteAway* obtains the last content word the user just types in and displays relevant SGPs instantly as the user writes away. The prototype system, *WriteAway*, is accessible at https://spg-write.herokuapp.com

53

The Companion Volume of the IJCNLP 2017 Proceedings: System Demonstrations, pages 53–56,
Taipei, Taiwan, November 27 – December 1, 2017. ©2017 AFNLP

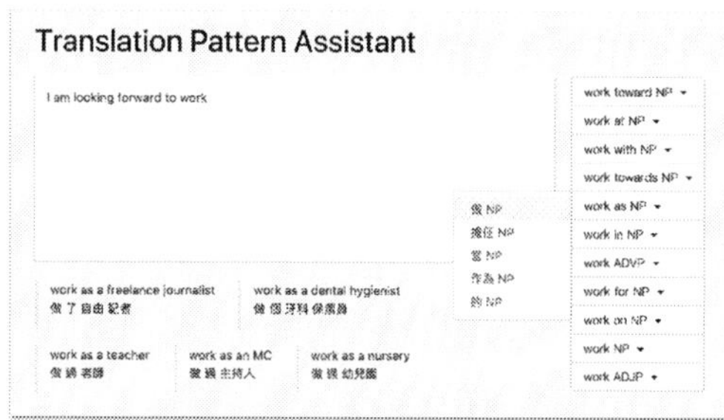

Figure 1: The prototype system, *WriteAway*

3 Extracting Synchronous Grammar Patterns

The extracting process involves recognizing the grammar patterns in the target language, aligning these patterns with their native language counterpart, and finally filtering valid SGPs with bilingual examples. We use a much simpler approach than previous work (Yen et al., 2015). We rely on a list of English grammar patterns from the HTML version of *COLLINS COBUILD GRAMMAR PATTERNS 1: VERBS* available at (http://arts-ccr-002.bham.ac.uk/ccr/patgram/). Therefore, the main focus is to identify the instances of these verb patterns and their counter part and to convert the counterpart instances into patterns.

3.1 Identifying English Grammar Patterns

In the identification process, we first use the GE-NIA Tagger (Tsuruoka et al., 2005) to shallow parse English sentences to obtain part of speech (POS) and chunk information ("B","I","O" symbols respectively indicate words at the beginning of a chunk, inside a chunk, and not part of NP, VP, ADJP, and ADVP).

Then, we identify head context words and elements of possible grammar patterns in the given sentences. Considering the input sentence "I apologize for my behavior.", we identify the verb "apologize" as a headword "V" followed by the preposition "for" and a noun phrase "V" 'my behavior' with 'n' based on the simple relation between the parse results and the notation of Pattern Grammar. In so doing, we identify an instance of the pattern "V for n" for headword "apologize", after we verify that this pattern can be found in *COLLINS COBUILD GRAMMAR PATTERNS 1: VERBS*. The phrase "apologize for my behavior" is retained for further processing (See Table 1).

Word	POS	B-I-O	Annotation	Pattern
I	PRP	B-NP		
apologize	VBP	B-VP	V	(V for n)
for	IN	B-PP	for	
my	PRP\$	B-NP	NP	
behavior	NN	I-NP	NP	
.	.	O		

Table 1: Anchor 'apologize for n' to a sentence

3.2 Align English Pattern to Chinese

After obtaining the target language grammar patterns and instances for each headword, we then proceed to extract the corresponding native language grammar pattern and its example instances.

For that, we use a Chinese word segment system, CKIP (Ma and Chen, 2003), to tokenize and tag Chinese sentence with POS information. We also use a word aligner, *fast_align* (Dyer et al., 2013) to explore the crossing-lingual relationship between the target language and native language words (e.g., English and Mandarin words). Finally, we convert the aligned native counterpart instances into grammar patterns.

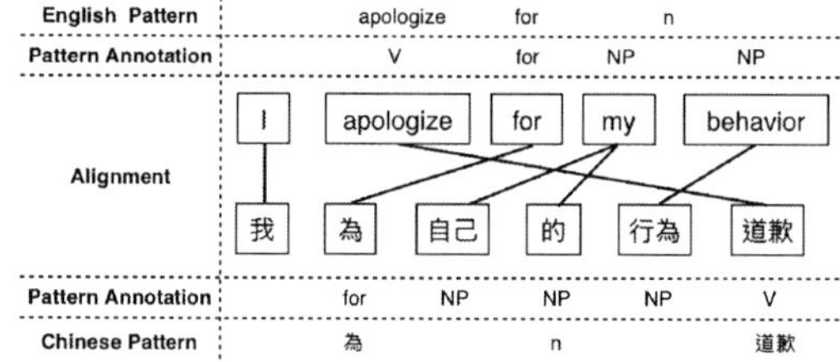

Figure 2: SGP and example phrase extraction according to alignment

See Figure 2 for an example of aligning "apologize: V for n" in a English sentence with its Chinese counterpart. When word alignment is 100% accurate, aligning and deriving synchronous patterns is straightforward. As shown in Figure 2, the headword "apologize" is aligned to "道歉", the preposition "for" to "為" and the noun phrase "my behavior" to "我的行為" converted to the same phrase label "n". Consequently, we can derive the SGP pair (e.g., "apologize for n", <"為 n 道歉">) from the aligned bilingual instance (e.g., "apologize for my behaviour", <"為自己的行為 道歉">).

However, word alignment is prone to errors, causing the SGP extraction process to derive erroneous results. Typically, a target-language word may be aligned incorrectly leading to incorrect links, missing links, or unnecessary links leading to an incorrectly identified counterpart instance and pattern.

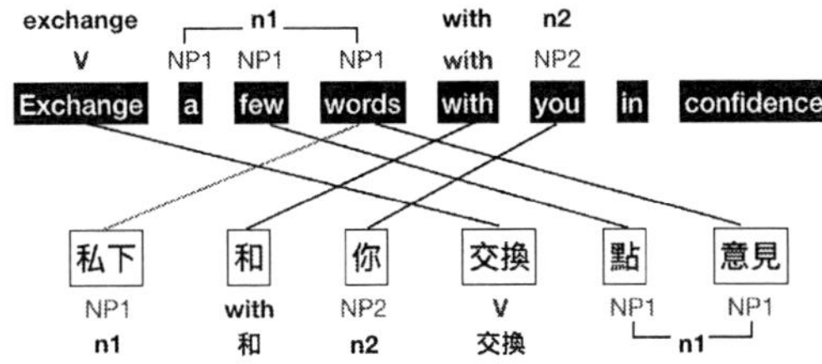

Figure 3: A SGP extraction failure

An example of word alignment error is shown in Figure 3. The pattern "exchange n1 with n2" is retrieved from sentence "I should like to exchange a few words with you in confidence . ". However, we derive an incorrect grammar pattern "n1 和 n2 交換 n1", caused by the incorrect alignments ("words", "私下"). If "words" is only related with "意見", we obtain the correct grammar pattern "和 n2 交換 n1" and bilingual example ("exchange a few words with you" "和你交換點意見").

To cope with word alignment errors, we stipulate that content phrase alignments are one-to-one. For one-to-two alignment, we select the longest consecutive Chinese segment (e.g., "點 意見"), and ignore the remaining disjoint segment (e.g., "私下") aligned to an English phrase chunk, because longer segments tend to be correct. With this method, we can let the noun phrase "a few words" only align to the Chinese phrase. In so doing, we can extract the correct Chinese grammar pattern "和 n2 交換 n1".

3.3   Re-rank the Chinese Pattern

Rank	Ch Template	Frequency	Instance
1	V n	15900	run for n, 競選 n
2	N n	2000	run for n, 競選 n
3	P n	1950	apologize for n, 向 n 道歉
4	n V	1900	apologize for n, n 道歉
5	D V n	1850	care for n, 來 照顧 n
6	V V n	1670	care for n, 負責 照顧 n
7	P V n	1400	run for n, 為了 競選 n
8	P n V	1390	apologize for n, 為 n 道歉

Table 2: The potential Chinese pattern templates for English pattern template 'V for n'

We designed a heuristic scoring scheme to re-rank the native-language patterns based on how likely are the specific template that match the pattern (see Table 2). We ask two linguistics students to come up with the scores for ranking of these templates. First, we generate T_{ET} a list of i most frequent Chinese patterns (templates), $t_1, t_2, t_3, \ldots, t_i$, for the English (template) ET, with frequency $F = f_1, f_2, f_3 \ldots, f_i$, is in descending order. These two annotators then assign a set of weight $W = w_1, w_2, w_3, \ldots, w_i$ such that the new order of re-ranked T_{ET} satisfy the expected rank $T_{ET-expected} = T_1, T_2, T_3, \ldots, T_i$ according to the weighted score, $w_1 * f_1, w_2 * f_2, w_3 * f_3, \ldots, w_i * f_i$, and then apply these weights to Chinese template instance. For example, based on these scores, we upgrade the ranks of the grammatical Chinese template 'V NP' and 'P NP V' , and degrade the ranks of the others tend to be ungrammatical. For example, we obtained the ranks of Chinese pattern template, [V n, P n V, N n, D V n, V V n, P V n, n V, P n] as the most likely top 8 Chinese templates for the English pattern 'V for n'. For the Chinese pattern template shown in Table 2, we can choose $w_3 = 0.3$, $w_4 = 0.5$, $w_8 = 5$ and otherwise 1 consistent with the expected ordering. Thus, we obtain a weight table for 'V for n' template. Finally, we multiply the frequency of each Chinese pattern by its weight in the weight table and re-rank for better results See Table 3 for an example re-ranking process of Chinese patterns of English pattern 'run for n'.

Ch Pattern (Template)	Frequency	Weighted Score	Rank
競選 n (V n)	36	36 * 1 = 36.0	1 ->1
參選 n (V n)	18	18 * 1 = 18.0	2 ->2
n 競選 (n V)	10	10 * 0.4 = 4.0	3 ->6
為 n (P n)	6	6 * 0.3 = 1.8	4 ->7
往 n 跑 (P n V)	2	2 * 5 = 10.0	5 ->3
為 n 奔波 (P n V)	1	1 * 5 = 5.0	6 ->4
為 n 跑 (P n V)	1	1 * 5 = 5.0	7 ->5

Table 3: rerank the Chinese patterns of 'run for n'

3.4   Selecting Good Example Phrases

In order to give concrete examples of these rather abstract synchronous grammar patterns, we extend the method described in (Kilgarriff et al., 2008) to select bilingual examples from the parallel corpus. The principles are as follows:

1. Correctness (English). The length of English pattern example multiplied by r must be similar with the length of the Chinese pattern example. Note that r is the average sentence length ratio between English and Chinese. This is to avoid selecting examples with word alignment errors.

2. Readability. Let l_E and l_C be the aver-

Annotation	Description	Count	Percentage
CC	Perfect	660	44.2%
CA	Good	82	5.5%
AA	Acceptable	300	20.1%
CI	ambivalent	7	0.5%
AI	Bad	91	6.1%
II	Incorrect	350	23.7%

Table 4: The evaluation result of sampled SGPs

age lengths of the English/Chinese pattern instances. We prefer bilingual examples of length closest to to l_E and l_C.

4 Evaluation

Our evaluation focused on verifying the correctness of extracted SGPs. First, we grouped SGPs by their corresponding English pattern templates. Next, we randomly sampled 10 English grammar patterns from each group along with top 5 corresponding Chinese grammar patterns. Then, we asked two linguisitcs to assess the appropriateness and quality of using the SGP for translation. In the assessment, each Chinese pattern is given a label of *(C)orrect, (A)cceptable* or *(I)ncorrect*. We evaluated a set of 1,497 Chinese grammar patterns for 31 different types of English patterns. Table 4 lists the counts and the proportion of the annotation results. There are 44% SGPs tagged with *CC*, 5.5% with *CA*, and 20% with *AA*. Overall, there are approximately 70% sampled SGPs are correct or acceptable.

In addition, we calculated the average score of the evaluation while assessing the scores of C = 2, A = 1 and I = 0. The average score is 1.2, which indicates that the results are only slightly better than acceptable, and obvious there is much room for improvement.

5 Conclusion and Future Work

In this paper, we have presented a method for automatically extracting Synchronous Grammar Patterns from a parallel corpus. The procedure involves extracting English patterns from parallel corpora, performing alignment of pattern sequences to Chinese sequences, generating and reranking counterpart Chinese patterns. The evaluation results show that our approach provides mostly correct or acceptable translation patterns that can be effectively exploited in assisted writing for second language learners. For that, we have also developed a prototype system so that ESL learners can write more confidently and frequently based on the synchronous grammar patterns displayed by the system.

We also conducted a preliminary investigation into the origins of incorrect SPGs and found that these errors were mainly due to alignment errors and segmentation errors. Moreover, idioms are usually hard to aligned and generalized into an SPG (e.g., "樂不思蜀" to "reluctant to leave"). Overall, common patterns with literal translation tend to lead to correct and useful SPGs for learner-writers, implying that a larger corpus can help producing more accurate SPGs. We will continue to work on the cases of SPG for nouns and adjectives.

References

Chris Dyer, Victor Chahuneau, and Noah A Smith. 2013. A simple, fast, and effective reparameterization of ibm model 2. Association for Computational Linguistics.

Susan Hunston and Gill Francis. 2000. Pattern grammar: A corpus-driven approach to the lexical grammar of english. *Computational Linguistics*, 27(2).

Adam Kilgarriff, Milos Husák, Katy McAdam, Michael Rundell, and Pavel Rychlý. 2008. Gdex: Automatically finding good dictionary examples in a corpus. In *Proc. Euralex*.

Wei-Yun Ma and Keh-Jiann Chen. 2003. Introduction to ckip chinese word segmentation system for the first international chinese word segmentation bakeoff. In *Proceedings of the second SIGHAN workshop on Chinese language processing-Volume 17*, pages 168–171. Association for Computational Linguistics.

Collins COBUILD Grammar Patterns. 1996. 1: Verbs. *Collins COBUILD, the University of Birmingham*.

Collins Cobuild Grammar Patterns. 1998. 2: Nouns and adjectives.

Yoshimasa Tsuruoka, Yuka Tateishi, Jin-Dong Kim, Tomoko Ohta, John McNaught, Sophia Ananiadou, and Jun'ichi Tsujii. 2005. Developing a robust part-of-speech tagger for biomedical text. In *Panhellenic Conference on Informatics*, pages 382–392. Springer.

Tzu-Hsi Yen, Jian-Cheng Wu, Jim Chang, Joanne Boisson, and Jason S Chang. 2015. Writeahead: Mining grammar patterns in corpora for assisted writing. In *ACL (System Demonstrations)*, pages 139–144.

Guess What:
A Question Answering Game via On-demand Knowledge Validation

Yu-Sheng Li
National Taiwan University
Taipei, Taiwan
b03902086@ntu.edu.tw

Chien-Hui Tseng
National Taiwan University
Taipei, Taiwan
r05725004@ntu.edu.tw

Chian-Yun Huang
National Chiao Tung University
Hsinchu, Taiwan
yun626.cs02@nctu.edu.tw

Wei-Yun Ma
Institute of Information Science, Academia Sinica
Taipei, Taiwan
ma@iis.sinica.edu.tw

Abstract

In this demo, we propose an idea of on-demand knowledge validation and fulfill the idea through an interactive Question-Answering (QA) game system, which is named Guess What. An object (e.g. dog) is first randomly chosen by the system, and then a user can repeatedly ask the system questions in natural language to guess what the object is. The system would respond with *yes/no* along with a confidence score. Some useful hints can also be given if needed. The proposed framework provides a pioneering example of on-demand knowledge validation in dialog environment to address such needs in AI agents/chatbots. Moreover, the released log data that the system gathered can be used to identify the most critical concepts/attributes of an existing knowledge base, which reflects human's cognition about the world.

1 Introduction and Script Outline

Knowledge validation (Merlevede and Vanthienen, 1991; Nazareth, 1989) aims to validate newly acquired knowledge. Most research work addresses the issue on text domain other than dialog environment. As the techniques and applications of AI agent and chatbot become mature and practical these days, the need of on-demand knowledge validation in the dialog environment is critical as the system needs to validate new knowledge acquired from users' words. Therefore we propose an interactive QA game between system and users, named Guess What[1] to fulfill the need in dialog environment. The demo presentation will be utilizing this web site to showcase our system in either Chinese or English version. Guess What is a variant of Twenty Questions game, which involves players taking the roles of the answerer and the questioners. The answerer chooses an object and conceal it to the other players. The questioners then ask *yes/no* questions to narrow down the wide range of the categories to which the object belongs. The question can be: "Is it animal?" or "Can it fly?", etc. The game terminates when the correct object is guessed by the questioners. Guess What is a kind of Chinese-based Twenty Questions game, where the system serves as the answerer and users as questioners. The answer set of the system currently contains 200 terms, which are general concepts such as dog, cat, boat, computer, etc. Figure 2 shows a running example of Guess What system.

The framework involves different research topics, such as question answering (Berant et al., 2013; Kwok et al., 2001) and relation prediction (Xu et al., 2016). The techniques include understanding the questions and identifying whether the object fits the description of the users' questions. Since most descriptions are based on the existence of a relationship between two entities, such as "Is it an animal?" or "Can it fly?", the latter mission turns out to be identifying whether a certain relationship between entities holds or not, which is a kind of on-demand knowledge validation.

Guess What goes through the following procedures: Parsing the user's question, followed by extracting knowledge and reasoning from metadata of Wikipedia[2] and a lexical semantic representation model named E-HowNet[3] (Ma and Chen, 2009; Chen et al., 2005). If the related knowledge

---

[1] http://guess-what.com.tw

[2] http://www.wikipedia.org/

[3] http://ehownet.iis.sinica.edu.tw/index.php

The Companion Volume of the IJCNLP 2017 Proceedings: System Demonstrations, pages 57–60,
Taipei, Taiwan, November 27 – December 1, 2017. ©2017 AFNLP

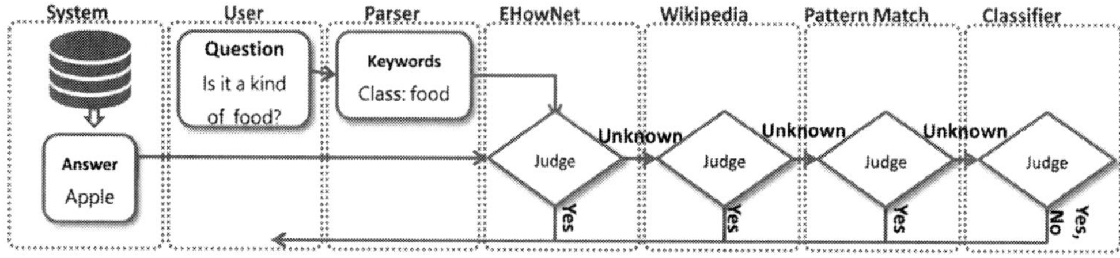

Figure 1: The process flow of Guess What system

Figure 2: A running example (screenshot) with lion as the answer in Guess What.

cannot be found, a pattern matching procedure and a classifier trained with online textual resources, such as Google Search results, are further applied. Figure 1 shows the process flow.

2 Question Understanding

In order to analyze the question, the system will parse the question through a Chinese parser, named CKIP parser[4], and the parsed question is then used to extract out a representative triple ⟨target, relation, withWhom⟩ via a set of extraction rules. The *target* is the answer term. The set of *relation*s consists of class, attribute, act, subject&act, act&object, location, and time. The *withWhom* is the corresponding term extracted from the question sentence which is in the certain relation to the target. Table 1 shows some examples of questions and their parsed triples where the answer is "bee."

3 Knowledge Validation

The following steps work with the triples parsed by the previous step, trying to figure out whether the relationship represented by each

[4]http://parser.iis.sinica.edu.tw/

Questions	Triples
Is it an animal?	⟨bee,class,animal⟩
Is it red?	⟨bee,attribute,red⟩
Can it fly?	⟨bee,act,fly⟩
Can it gather food?	⟨bee,act&obj, gather&food⟩

Table 1: Questions and their parsed triples

triple holds or not. For example, for the question "Can it gather food?", its triple is "⟨bee,act&object,gather&food⟩", Our goal is to validate the triple.

3.1 E-HowNet

3.1.1 Introduction

Extended-HowNet (E-HowNet) is a frame-based entity-relation model in Chinese and English, annotated by hand. Currently there are more than 100,000 entities in E-HowNet. Take bee for example. The definition of bee on E-HowNet is { InsectWorm : predication = { gather : theme = { food : source = { FlowerGrass } } , agent = { ∼ } } }, as illustrated in Figure 3.

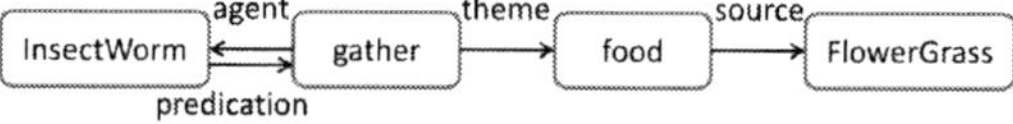

Figure 3: Graphical illustration of definition of bee

The above structure can be phrased in natural language as "bee is an insect whose predication is to gather food from flower." Here we ignore the actual definition of InsectWorm and FlowerGrass for simplicity, and the term *agent* means that bees are the subject of the action gather. The ∼ symbol refers backwards to InsectWorm in this case.

3.1.2 Usage

We first use E-HowNet to validate if two entities have a certain relation. For example, for relation "act," , we check out whether there is some predication link to the withWhom term in the E-HowNet definition of the answer. Furthermore, for relation "actobject", we examine if there is some theme or patient link to the withWhom term. Since E-HowNet contains less information about time and location, E-HowNet is not used for the two types of relations.

3.2 Wikipedia

E-HowNet can provide a certain level of common sense, and it sometimes still lack comprehensive common sense and some necessary domain knowledge in order to validate the given questions. This is where Wikipedia can bring the contribution. For almost every Wikipedia title, there are some related categorical hyperlinks at the bottom. If we build edges between these hyperlinked pages and regard the whole Wikipedia categorical hyperlinks as a graph, any given triple can also be validated through the graph. For instance, in the page of bat[5] there are

Bats ; Animal flight ; Pollinators ; Night ; Cave organisms ; Extant Ypresian first appearances ; Animals that use echolocation

Now we know that bats can fly, can pollinate, might be nocturnal, might live in caves, and can use echolocation. Moreover, these are not merely class-type categories, but also information about ability, location, etc.

3.3 From Online Search Texts

The information in knowledge bases is relatively refined but limited while the content on the Internet is relatively rich. Therefore, when searching the knowledge bases is insufficient to claim the relationship between the entities pair doesn't exist, we turn to online resources for more information. For each term in the answer set of the system, we collect textual data from the following sources:

1. top 10 pages of Google search results with the answer term as the query

2. the article of the answer term in Wikipedia

3. the article of the answer term in Baidu Baike[6]

4. the sentences containing the answer term in Academia Sinica Balanced Corpus (ASBC) [7]

With the help of these data, we apply pattern matching and use a classifier to check whether the relationship between the target and withWhom term holds or not.

- SVM Classifier
  We regard the validation of the relationship represented in the triple as a binary classification problem with two classes, *yes* and *no*. For each triple, we extract four features from the textual resource about the target term. There is no difference in different relations in the way extracting features. The four features are listed below.

  Denote $term_q$ = withWhom, $term_a$ = target. Define the the distance of two terms to be the number of words between them

  1. Proportional frequency: Number of sentences containing $term_q$ divided by total number of sentences.
  2. Average distance of $term_a$ and $term_q$
  3. Shortest distance of $term_a$ and $term_q$
  4. Word vectors similarity: By utilizing the word vector model (word2Vec package)[8] trained with ASBC corpus, we can get the vectors in 300 dimensions of terms. We compute the cosine similarity between vectors of $term_a$ and $term_q$ as a feature.

4 Experiments and Discussion

In order to evaluate the performance of each component in the procedure, we designed a testing set with 792 ⟨question, answer, *yes/no*⟩ triples, such as ⟨Is it an animal, monkey, *yes*⟩. There are 112 distinct answers and each answer is paired with about 7 questions on average, where questions are manually generated. There are 208 *yes*-labeled and 584 *no*-labeled triples in this testing set. Different kinds of relations are included in these questions as shown in table 2.

Type	class	attr.	act	location	total
Number	181	304	246	61	792

Table 2: Number of each type of questions

[5]http://en.wikipedia.org/wiki/Bat
[6]http://baike.baidu.com/
[7]http://asbc.iis.sinica.edu.tw/
[8]https://code.google.com/archive/p/word2vec/

Table 3 shows performance of each component in our experiments. From the table we can find that E-HowNet, Wikipedia and pattern matching have high precision but low recall, while classifier has relatively low precision and high recall. In summary, in the whole process, E-HowNet, Wikipedia, and pattern matching will be applied first to give reliable predictions. If the corresponding information is not found, the classifier will compensate for the recall. As a result, the whole process achieved the best F1-score.

	Precision	Recall	F1-score
E-HowNet	0.9158	0.4183	0.5743
Wikipedia	1.0000	0.0962	0.1754
Pattern	0.9500	0.0913	0.1667
Classifier	0.7135	0.6587	0.6850
Overall	0.7585	0.7548	0.7566

Table 3: Performance of each component

5 Log Analysis

The system records every question asked by users. Since the latest version of the system was launched, we have recorded 667 games, which contain 5016 questions in total. After removing 277 illegal question sentences (which don't contain 'it' in the sentence) and 274 direct answer term matching, there are 4465 questions in remaining. There are 257 distinct users (identified by their IP addresses) and each user played 2.6 games on average. We summarize the first question which users tend to ask in the game. The top frequently asked types of questions are shown in Table 4, which reflects the most critical concepts/attributes of human's mind.

6 Conclusion

The game system presented in this paper involves a mixture of information extraction techniques. The main contributions include being as a pioneering example of on-demand knowledge validation in dialog environment to address such needs in AI agents/chatbots, and comprehensive analysis of the log data, which can be used to guide the construction of a new knowledge base or be used to identify the most critical concepts/attributes of an existing knowledge based to reflect human's cognition about the world. In the future, we will work on expanding the existing answer set and further develop knowledge inference

Rank	Type	Examples	Count
1	human beings	Is it human?	96
2	animal	Is it a kind of animal?	59
3	food	Is it a kind of food? Is it edible?	59
4	living beings	Is it a kind of living beings? Is it alive?	50
5	fly	Can it fly?	10
6	occupation	Is it a kind of occupation?	4
7	thing	Is it a kind of thing?	4
8	plant	Is it a kind of plant?	3

Table 4: Types of questions frequently asked as the first one in the game

mechanisms to utilize indirect evidences with the online textual data.

References

Jonathan Berant, Andrew Chou, Roy Frostig, and Percy Liang. 2013. Semantic parsing on freebase from question-answer pairs. In *EMNLP*, volume 2, page 6.

Keh-Jiann Chen, Shu-Ling Huang, Yueh-Yin Shih, and Yi-Jun Chen. 2005. Extended-hownet-a representational framework for concepts. In *OntoLex 2005-Ontologies and Lexical Resources IJCNLP-05 Workshop*.

Cody Kwok, Oren Etzioni, and Daniel S Weld. 2001. Scaling question answering to the web. *ACM Transactions on Information Systems (TOIS)*, 19(3):242–262.

Wei-Yun Ma and Keh-Jiann Chen. 2009. Lexical semantic representation and semantic composition: An introduction to e-hownet. Technical report, CKIP Group, Academia Sinica.

P Merlevede and Jan Vanthienen. 1991. A structured approach to formalization and validation of knowledge. In *Developing and Managing Expert System Programs, 1991., Proceedings of the IEEE/ACM International Conference on*, pages 149–158. IEEE.

Derek L Nazareth. 1989. Issues in the verification of knowledge in rule-based systems. *International Journal of Man-Machine Studies*, 30(3):255–271.

Yan Xu, Ran Jia, Lili Mou, Ge Li, Yunchuan Chen, Yangyang Lu, and Zhi Jin. 2016. Improved relation classification by deep recurrent neural networks with data augmentation. *arXiv preprint arXiv:1601.03651*.

STCP: Simplified-Traditional Chinese Conversion and Proofreading

Jiarui Xu[1] and **Xuezhe Ma**[1] and **Chen-Tse Tsai**[2] and **Eduard Hovy**[1]

1 Language Technologies Institute, Carnegie Mellon University

2 Department of Computer Science, University of Illinois at Urbana-Champaign

{jiaruix, xuezhem}@cs.cmu.edu, ctsai12@illinois.edu, hovy@cmu.edu

Abstract

This paper aims to provide an effective tool for conversion between Simplified Chinese and Traditional Chinese. We present STCP, a customizable system comprising statistical conversion model, and proofreading web interface. Experiments show that our system achieves comparable character-level conversion performance with the state-of-art systems. In addition, our proofreading interface can effectively support diagnostics and data annotation. STCP is available at http://lagos.lti.cs.cmu.edu:8002/

1 Introduction

There are two standard character sets of the contemporary Chinese written language: Simplified Chinese and Traditional Chinese. Simplified Chinese is officially used in mainland China and Singapore, while Traditional Chinese is used in Taiwan, Hong Kong, and Macau. The conversion has become an essential problem with the increasing communication and collaboration among Chinese-speaking regions.

Although several conversion systems have been made available to the public, the conversion problem, however, remains unsolved. In this paper, we present an open-source system that provides a statistical model for conversion, as well as a web interface for proofreading. Our system achieves comparable performance with state-of-art systems. To the best of our knowledge, it is the first open-source statistical conversion system.

Another contribution of our system is the proofreading web interface. It is important for users to proofread the converted result and to make edits based on the linguistic information.

2 Levels of Conversion

Halpern and Kerman (1999) discussed the pitfalls and complexities of Chinese-to-Chinese conversion and introduced four conversion levels: code level, orthographic level, lexemic level, and contextual level, respectively. In this paper, we compact them into two levels of conversion: character level and cord level.

2.1 Character level

There exists a mapping between Simplified Chinese characters and Traditional Chinese characters. Most characters only have a single corresponding character, while some characters may have multiple corresponding characters. In Simplified-to-Traditional conversion, characters with one-to-many mappings constitute about 12% of commonly used Chinese characters (Halpern and Kerman, 1999). Such phenomenon exists in Traditional-to-Simplified as well but to a much lesser extent. Character-level conversion of a given sentence involves both replacing characters that have one-to-one mapping with corresponding characters and disambiguating characters that have one-to-many mappings.

2.2 Word level

A concept may have different string surfaces due to the differences in word usage among various Chinese-speaking areas. For example, ⚽ is referred to as "football" in British English but "soccer ball" in American English. Such phenomenon is quite typical in Chinese-speaking areas. For example, Sydney is 悉尼 in mainland China but 雪梨 in Taiwan. Word-level conversion of a sentence involves determining if a word should be replaced with a corresponding word in look-up table. Disambiguation is also necessary if there are multiple corresponding words.

61

The Companion Volume of the IJCNLP 2017 Proceedings: System Demonstrations, pages 61–64,
Taipei, Taiwan, November 27 – December 1, 2017. ©2017 AFNLP

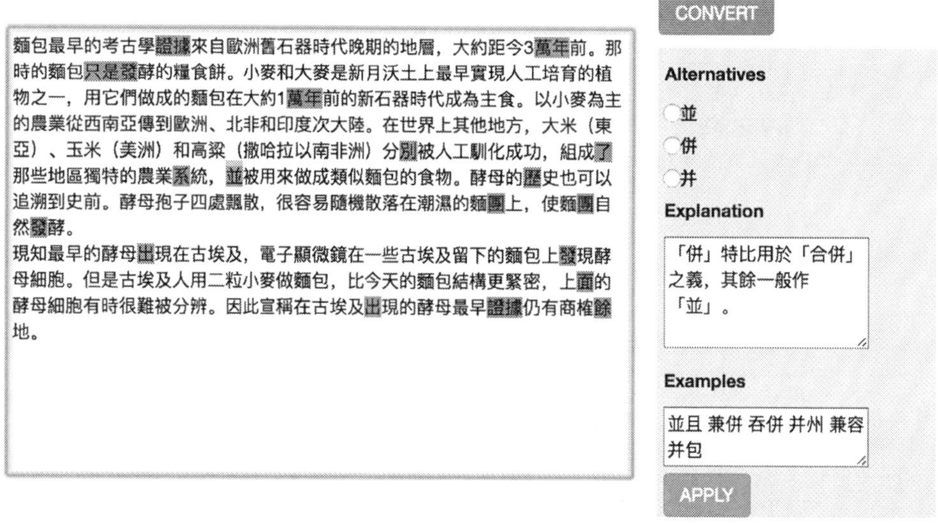

Figure 1: Screenshot of proofreading interface

We use the following sentence in Simplified Chinese to elaborate the conversion process:

我	了解	云端	软件
I	know	cloud	software

Based on look-up tables of the character mappings, we list characters with one-to-one mappings in the above example sentence in Table 1 and those with one-to-many mappings in Table 2 Word mapping is shown in Table 3.

SC	我	解	端	软	件
TC	我	解	端	軟	件

Table 1: one-to-one character mapping

SC	TC	English
了	了	(auxiliary)
	瞭	know
云	云	say
	雲	cloud

Table 2: one-to-many character mapping

SC	软件
TC	軟體

Table 3: Word mapping in example sentence.

We decide to replace '软件' with '軟體' and finally get the target sentence in Traditional Chinese: 我瞭解雲端軟體

3 System Architecture

3.1 Model

The Simplified-Traditional conversion problem is formulated as a translation problem (Brown et al., 1990):

Given a sentence s from source language (e.g. Simplified Chinese), return a sentence t in target language (e.g. Traditional Chinese) that maximizes the conditional probability:

$$P(t|s) = \frac{P(t)P(s|t)}{P(s)} \propto P(t)P(s|t)$$

Here we let $P(s|t)$ be the same for any candidate sentence t. Therefore, $P(t|s) \propto P(t)$ and the goal is to find:

$$t^* = \underset{t}{\mathrm{argmax}} P(t)$$

We describe how to generate candidate sentences through word and character conversion in section 3.1.1 and 3.1.2. The language model we used is briefly introduced in section 3.1.3.

3.1.1 Word Conversion

We tokenize the source sentence s into word sequence w_1, w_2, ..., w_n. In our system, we use Jieba[1] Chinese text segmentation. For each word

---

[1] https://github.com/fxsjy/jieba

w_i, if there exists a mapping of w_i in mapping table, we convert w_i into word w_i' in target language.

3.1.2 Character Conversion

After word conversion, the characters in words that have not been converted have one-to-one or one-to-many mapping. We generate candidate set T that contains all possible sentences by combining every possible conversions of each character.

3.1.3 Language Model

By default, the system uses a character-level language model with order of 5, estimated by KenLM (Heafield, 2011; Heafield et al., 2013). We choose KenLM because of its advantage in time and storage efficiency. User can substitute it with other trained language model.

3.2 Proofreading Interface

We provide a web-based proofreading interface that allows users to correct the converted text. Automatic conversion between Simplified Chinese and Traditional Chinese can never achieve 100% accuracy and we believe that, in many scenarios, such as government, commercial and legal document conversion, it is important to convert all characters and words as accurately as possible. Characters and words that have alternatives will be highlighted. When user selects these ambiguous fragments, explanation and example will be displayed and user can easily choose an alternative to replace the automatic results. Example proofreading of a paragraph and its highlights are shown in Figure 1.

4 Experimentation

Ministry of Education of the P.R.C. and Chinese Information Processing Society of China held a competition on the Evaluation of Intelligent Conversion System of Simplified Chinese and Traditional Chinese [2] (MOE-CIPSC) in 2013. There are two core tasks: Character Conversion and Terminology Conversion. Few high-quality parallel corpus is available (Chang and Kung, 2007) and it is expensive to build one. Most websites that claim to have both Simplified Chinese and Traditional Chinese versions are using automatic systems without proofreading, thus are prone to errors. Our evaluation strategy adopts the task one of MOE evaluation.

4.1 Data

We use the Chinese Gigaword Fifth Edition (Parker et al., 2011) produce by the Linguistic Data Consortium (LDC). We select documents of type 'story' from Central News Agency (CMA), Taiwan after 2004, which are written in Traditional Chinese. In order to evaluate character conversion, we need to assume that there is no difference in word usage. Since conversion from Traditional Chinese to Simplified Chinese is not problematic on character level(Halpern and Kerman, 1999), we convert the CMA corpus into Simplified Chinese and use it as source language text set. The original CMA corpus becomes the target language text set. We split the entire data set into 80% training and 20% testing data randomly.

4.2 Evaluation

MOE-CIPSC evaluation provides a list of characters that have one-to-many mapping[3]. Overall accuracy is defined as: (#correctly converted ambiguous characters) / (#ambiguous characters). We also use Macro-average accuracy to evaluate performance across different characters.

4.3 Results and Analysis

Accuracies on character conversion are reported in Table 4 and Table 5. Note that XMUCC is a pre-trained system and OpenCC is a rule-based system. STCP outperforms OpenCC in terms of both accuracies and achieved comparable accuracy with XMUCC. Comparisons of these system are in section 5.

	OpenCC	XMUCC	STCP
Overall Accuracy	98.90	99.81	99.64

Table 4: Overall accuracies

	OpenCC	XMUCC	STCP
Macro-avg Acc.	91.75	96.98	95.73

Table 5: Macro-average accuracies

5 Related Work

There are several statistical approaches that have been proposed. Chen et al. (2011) integrates statistical features, including language models and lex-

---

[2]http://www.moe.edu.cn/s78/A19/A19_
gggs/s8478/201302/t20130225_181150.html

[3]http://bj.bcebos.com/cips-upload/dzb.
txt

ical semantic consistencies, into log-linear models. Li et al. (2010) uses look-up tables retrieved from Wikipedia to perform word substitution and disambiguate characters through language model. We adopt this method to build our conversion model. We use different look-up tables and we use higher order language model while they only use bigram and unigram.

The four most popular and publicly available systems are Google Translate, Microsoft Translator, Open Chinese Convert (OpenCC), and a system co-developed by Xiamen University, Ministry of Education of The People's Republic of China, and Beijing Normal University (XMUCC). OpenCC [4] is an open-source project that performs conversion based on lookup tables constructed manually. XMUCC [5] integrates language models and lexical semantic consistencies into log-linear models (Chen et al., 2011). However, XMUCC can be accessed through web interface and but it can only be executed in Windows command line as standalone program.

In end-use applications, especially when high quality conversion is required, human proofreading is required. Compared to (Zhang, 2011, 2014), our conversion is based on language model, instead of simply choosing the most frequent target characters. In addition, our proofreading interface highlights not only ambiguous characters, but also words. Users can also customize the system by importing look-up tables and language model, which can be useful for particular domains, such as science, business, and law.

6   Conclusion and Future Work

We develop an open-source customizable Chinese conversion system that is based on look-up tables and language model with a proofreading interface that assists end-use application. For future work, we will experiment with different language modeling approaches, such as neural language model. We will use the proofreading interface to construct parallel corpus of high quality to evaluate word-level conversion.

Acknowledgments

References

Peter F. Brown, John Cocke, Stephen A. Della Pietra, Vincent J. Della Pietra, Fredrick Jelinek, John D. Lafferty, Robert L. Mercer, and Paul S. Roossin. 1990. A statistical approach to machine translation. *Comput. Linguist.* 16(2):79–85. http://dl.acm.org/citation.cfm?id=92858.92860.

Jing-Shin Chang and Chun-Kai Kung. 2007. A chinese-to-chinese statistical machine translation model for mining synonymous simplified-traditional chinese terms. *Proceedings of Machine Translation Summit XI* .

Yidong Chen, Xiaodong Shi, and Changle Zhou. 2011. A simplified-traditional chinese character conversion model based on log-linear models. In *2011 International Conference on Asian Language Processing*. pages 3–6. https://doi.org/10.1109/IALP.2011.15.

Jack Halpern and Jouni Kerman. 1999. Pitfalls and complexities of chinese to chinese conversion. In *International Unicode Conference (14th) in Boston*.

Kenneth Heafield. 2011. Kenlm: Faster and smaller language model queries. In *Proceedings of the Sixth Workshop on Statistical Machine Translation*. Association for Computational Linguistics, pages 187–197.

Kenneth Heafield, Ivan Pouzyrevsky, Jonathan H Clark, and Philipp Koehn. 2013. Scalable modified kneser-ney language model estimation. In *Proceedings of the 51st Annual Meeting of the Association for Computational Linguistics*. pages 690–696.

Min-Hsiang Li, Shih-Hung Wu, Yi-Ching Zeng, Ping-che Yang, and Tsun Ku. 2010. Chinese characters conversion system based on lookup table and language model. *Computational Linguistics and Chinese Language Processing* 15(1):19–36.

Robert Parker, David Graff, Junbo Kong, Ke Chen, and Kazuaki Maeda. 2011. English gigaword fifth edition LDC2011T07. DVD. *Philadelphia: Linguistic Data Consortium* .

Xiaoheng Zhang. 2011. A simplified-traditional chinese conversion tool with a supporting environment for human proofreading. *The 11th Chinese National Conference on Computational Linguistics, CNCCL* .

Xiaoheng Zhang. 2014. *A Comparative Study on Simplified-Traditional Chinese Translation*, Springer International Publishing, Cham, pages 212–222. https://doi.org/10.1007/978-3-319-12277-9_19.

---

[4] https://github.com/BYVoid/OpenCC

[5] http://jf.cloudtranslation.cc/

Deep Neural Network based system for solving Arithmetic Word problems

Purvanshi Mehta *
Thapar University

Pruthwik Mishra * and **Vinayak Athavale**
Language Technologies Research Center
IIIT HYDERABAD

Manish Shrivastava and **Dipti Misra Sharma**
Language Technologies Research Center
IIIT HYDERABAD

Abstract

This paper presents DILTON, a system which solves simple arithmetic word problems. DILTON first predicts the operation that is to be performed ('-','+','*','/') through a deep neural network based model and then uses it to generate the answer. DILTON divides the question into two parts - worldstate and query as shown in Figure 1. The worldstate and the query are processed separately in two different networks and finally the networks are merged to predict the final operation. DILTON learns to predict operations with 88.81 % in a corpus of primary school questions. With simple similarity between the contexts of quantities appearing in the problem and the question text, we are able to identify 92.25 % of relevant quantities and solve 81% of the questions. Our code and data is publicly available.[1]

1 Introduction

In recent years there is a growing interest in understanding and generating natural language for the purpose of answering questions related to science and maths. Computers are better than humans in terms of both speed and accuracy at mathematical calculations but it is still a challenging task for computers to solve even elementary grade math-word-problems (Problems described in natural language). From the perspective of Natural Language Processing, mathematical word problems are challenging to solve as we need to reduce the natural language text to a set of equations which we can then automatically solve.

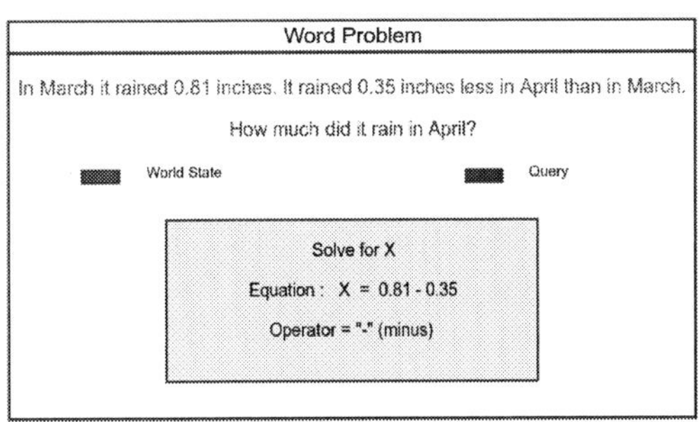

Figure 1: Example problem and answer generation

Arithmetic word problems can be solved with the help of the numbers mentioned in the text and their relationships through basic mathematical operations (addition, subtraction, division, multiplication). Arithmetic word problems begin by describing a partial world state, followed by simple updates and end with a quantitative question. For humans, understanding the language part is trivial, but the reasoning may be challenging; for computers, the opposite is true. Designing algorithms to automatically solve math and science problems is a long-standing AI challenge (Bobrow, 1964). Work done in this domain range from template-matching to narrative-building, integer linear programming and factorization. In symbolic approaches, math problem sentences are transformed by pattern matching or verb categorization. Equations are derived from the patterns. Statistical learning methods are employed in the paper (Hosseini et al., 2014) There has been work done in extracting units and rates of quantities (Roy et al., 2015); (Mitra and Baral, 2016) focus on addition-subtraction problems. We focus on solving problems with a single operation, (Koncel-Kedziorski et al., 2015) focus on single equation problems, and (Hosseini et al., 2014) focus on al-

---

* denotes equal contribution

[1]https://github.com/ijcnlp2017anonsubmission/Dilton-word-problem-solver

The Companion Volume of the IJCNLP 2017 Proceedings: System Demonstrations, pages 65–68,
Taipei, Taiwan, November 27 – December 1, 2017. ©2017 AFNLP

gebra word problems.

Our system used GRUs and LSTMs to process the question and predicted the operation between the numbers mentioned in the text. Arithmetic word problems concisely describe a world state(WorldState) and pose questions(Query) about it. For example, Figure 1 shows one such problem. The described state can be modeled with a system of equations whose solution specifies the question's answer.

This paper studies the task of learning to automatically solve such problems given only the natural language with two operands in the question. The solution involves the understanding of the text. In our system, first of the question is divided into two parts WorldState(describes the quantities and how are they being modified) and Query(The quantity being asked). The WorldState and the Query are processed separately.

Our contributions are -

1. We present DILTON , a novel, fully automated system that learns to solve arithmetic word problems with two operators.

2. We used a Deep Neural Network based model to automatically predict the mathematical operation present in a arithmetic word problem.

3. We propose a simple and effective way of identifying relevant quantities in a word problem through similarity between context of each quantity and the corresponding question.

Problem Description

We address the problem of automatically solving arithmetic word problems. The input to our system is the problem text P , which mentions 2 quantities num1, num2 . Our goal is to predict the operation between the two numerical quantities. Inputs to our model are in the form of a question which consists of a world state which describes the background of the question and a query which describes the quantity for which the question is being asked.

2 System Working

DILTON's working is shown in figure 3. Input as the math word problem is given and then the numerical quantities are separated from the text. Word problem is separated into query and the world state. The world state is defined as the word problem without the final query which has information required to answer the query. We vectorized both the query, worldstate separately and then used our Deep Neural Network based model to predict the operation needed to answer the query. After predicting the operation the system applied it on the numerical operands to compute the answer to the problem.

3 Model
3.1 Architecture:
Out system is a pipeline consisting of three different modules that are detailed below.

3.2 Sequence Autoencoder
We used word2vec (Mikolov et al., 2013) to convert each word in the world state, query to its vector representation. We then used a sequence autoencoder (Dai and Le, 2015) with a GRU to encode both the world state and the query separately.

3.3 Combining the representations
We take the outputs of the sequence autoencoder for both the query, world state separately and combine them by doing an element wise sum.

3.4 Predicting the answer
We take the combined representation and then apply a GRU on it to get a vector representation for the combined (query,world state) The terminal layer in our architecture is a fully connected layer. It converts the output of GRU-RNN layer into softmax probabilities for each class.

3.5 Operand Prediction
In order to find the operands in a word problem, we need to first filter out irrelevant quantities. e.g John has 3 pens and 2 pencils. Jane have John 5 more pens. How many pens John have now? In this question, the quantity 2 is irrelevant which can be easily found out by a similarity match between the context of the quantity and the question asked. We experimented with different context window lengths across quantities and reported the results.

3.6 Training
We train this whole network end to end by using categorical cross entropy error and stochastic gradient descent. We use 30% Dropouts (Srivastava et al., 2014) for regularization and to prevent overfitting. We used 50 sized word2vec (Mikolov et al., 2013) embeddings and GRU's with 100 hidden nodes to encode both query, worldstate and trained the network for 40 epochs.

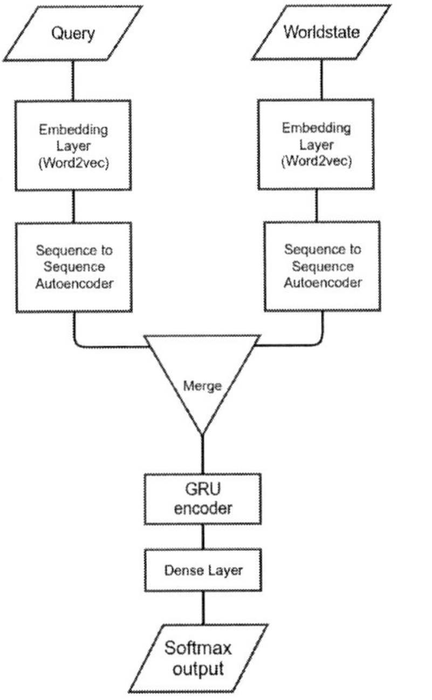

Figure 2: DILTON network

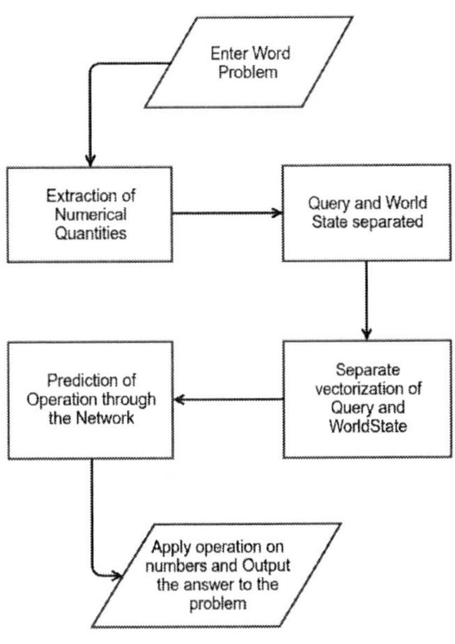

Figure 3: Workflow of DILTON

4   Experimental Study

In this section, we seek to validate our proposed modeling. We evaluate our systems performance based on the percentage of correct operator prediction. We do not directly evaluate our systems ability to map raw text segments into our representation, but instead evaluate this capability extrinsically, in the context of the aforementioned task, since good standardization is necessary to perform quantitative inference.

5   Experimental Setup Dataset

We have used the dataset provided by MAWPS (Koncel-Kedziorski et al., 2016). The dataset consists of the dataset included in singleop and addsub domain. The dataset consists of questions with two operands on which basic operations (addition, subtraction, multiplication, division) can be performed.These datasets have similar problem types, but have different characteristics. Problem types include combinations of additions, subtractions, one unknown equation, and U.S. money word problems. We randomly split the dataset into a dev set (for algorithm design, parameter tuning and debugging) and a test set. Our training set consists of 1314 questions and test set consists of 438 questions.

6   Baseline methods

We compare our approach with ARIS(Hosseini et al., 2014). The comparisons are mentioned in the table. Our system performs better than ARIS(Hosseini et al., 2014) in case when the question consists of two operands and a single operator. The neural networks performs better in case of learning the operations to be performed.

7   Evaluation Metrics

We get a training accuracy of 99.01%. and an accuracy of 88.81% on our testing data. We compare our results with ARIS which consisted of 395 questions and predicted the operations thorough verb categorization. ARIS dataset consists of 186 questions which our system cannot handle at the moment because three operators are present in the question. We compared our system against the 209 problems with single operation in the ARIS dataset.

8   Results

We evaluate DILTON in solving arithmetic problems in the dataset [2] provided by SingleOp

---

[2] We have not included the questions which had more than two numerical quantities

Table 1:   Accuracies when trained on different models

Model	Training	Testing
GRU	99.54	88.81
LSTM	98.33	87.90

and AddSub dataset . AddSub dataset was used by Aris(Hosseini et al., 2014) that achieved an accuracy of 81.2% for sentence categorization. DILTON shows significant improvement over their accuracies. It can learn to solve arithmetic word problems with an accuracy 88.81% on our testing data on a dataset consists of single basic operation.

Table 2: Comparison results

System	Categorization accuracies(%)
Aris	81.2
DILTON	88.81

We do not include the questions which consists of more than two numbers. We predict the final operator(addition, subtraction, multiplication, division) rather than categorizing every verb.

9   Error Analysis

DILTON encounters following errors while solving word problems:-

1. Questions which consist of more than two numerical values.

2. Question such as Raman had 2 chocolates and 4 apples. How many chocolates did Raman had? It cannot identify that there is no relation between 2 chocolates and 4 apples. Adding one more category of no relation can solve this.

10   Conclusion & Future Work

We propose a Deep learning based architecture on the task of math word problem solving. We divide the question such that the knowledge about the entities and the quantities asked are separated. Processing them separately makes sure that they don't share the same word embeddings. We show that deep learning models can significantly outperform many other approaches involving rule based systems or template matching or even traditional machine learning based approaches. As future work we will try to include the questions which can handle irrelevant information and questions with more than two numerical values.

Table 3: Quantity Identification and Equation Formation Accuracy

Context Window Length	Quantity	Equation
1	92.25	81.92
2	79.35	70.47
3	77.74	69.04

References

Daniel G Bobrow. 1964. Natural language input for a computer problem solving system.

Andrew M Dai and Quoc V Le. 2015. Semi-supervised sequence learning. In *Advances in Neural Information Processing Systems*, pages 3079–3087.

Mohammad Javad Hosseini, Hannaneh Hajishirzi, Oren Etzioni, and Nate Kushman. 2014. Learning to solve arithmetic word problems with verb categorization. In *EMNLP*, pages 523–533.

Rik Koncel-Kedziorski, Hannaneh Hajishirzi, Ashish Sabharwal, Oren Etzioni, and Siena Dumas Ang. 2015. Parsing algebraic word problems into equations. *Transactions of the Association for Computational Linguistics*, 3:585–597.

Rik Koncel-Kedziorski, Subhro Roy, Aida Amini, Nate Kushman, and Hannaneh Hajishirzi. 2016. Mawps: A math word problem repository. In *HLT-NAACL*, pages 1152–1157.

Tomas Mikolov, Ilya Sutskever, Kai Chen, Greg S Corrado, and Jeff Dean. 2013. Distributed representations of words and phrases and their compositionality. In *Advances in neural information processing systems*, pages 3111–3119.

Arindam Mitra and Chitta Baral. 2016. Learning to use formulas to solve simple arithmetic problems. In *ACL (1)*.

Subhro Roy, Tim Vieira, and Dan Roth. 2015. Reasoning about quantities in natural language. *Transactions of the Association for Computational Linguistics*, 3:1–13.

Nitish Srivastava, Geoffrey E Hinton, Alex Krizhevsky, Ilya Sutskever, and Ruslan Salakhutdinov. 2014. Dropout: a simple way to prevent neural networks from overfitting. *Journal of machine learning research*, 15(1):1929–1958.

Author Index

Alva-Manchego, Fernando, 1
Apostolidis, Lazaros, 21
Athavale, Vinayak, 65

Burchfield, Deana, 5

Carrell, Annabelle, 5
Chaloux, Julianne, 5
Chang, Jason, 49, 53
Chang, Jim, 53
Chen, Chun-Hsun, 17
Chen, Jhih-Jie, 49, 53
Chen, Tongfei, 5
Chen, Yidong, 29
Choi, Su Jeong, 9
Comerford, Alex, 5
Costello, Cash, 5

Dredze, Mark, 5
Du, Jinhua, 33
Duh, Kevin, 5

Finin, Tim, 5

Georgakopoulos Kolaitis, Spiros, 21
Glass, Benjamin, 5

Han, Jen-Chieh, 17
Hao, Shudong, 5
Harman, Craig, 5
Hovy, Eduard, 61
Hsieh, Shu-Kai, 41
Hu, Jinming, 29
Huang, Chian-Yun, 57

Koehn, Philipp, 5
Kompatsiaris, Yiannis, 21
Kuo, Min-Feng, 17

Lam, Chun Yin, 45
Lau, Tak On, 45
Lawrie, Dawn, 5
Le-Hong, Phuong, 37
Lee, John, 45
Lee, Po-Ching, 17
Li, Bing, 45

Li, Keying, 45
Li, Liangyou, 33
Li, Yu-Sheng, 57
Liakata, Maria, 21, 41
Lippincott, Tom, 5
Liu, Meichun, 45
Liu, Qun, 33

Ma, Wei-Yun, 57
Ma, Xuezhe, 61
Martín Wanton, Tamara, 25
Martin, Patrick, 5
May, Chandler, 5
Mayfield, James, 5
Mehta, Purvanshi, 65
Miller, Scott, 5
Mishra, Pruthwik, 65

Nguyen, Tuan Anh, 37
Noh, Yunseok, 9

Paetzold, Gustavo, 1
Palmero Aprosio, Alessio, 25
Pan, Chao-Lin, 13
Papadopoulos, Symeon, 21
Park, Se-Young, 9
Park, Seong-Bae, 9
Peinelt, Nicole, 41
Pham, Hoang, 37
Poliak, Adam, 5
Procter, Rob, 21

Rastogi, Pushpendre, 5

Sankepally, Rashmi, 5
Scarton, Carolina, 25
Sharma, Dipti, 65
Shi, Xiaodong, 29
Shih, Chao-Chuang, 17
Shrivastava, Manish, 65
Specia, Lucia, 1, 25

Tan, Zhixing, 29
Thomas, Max, 5
Tonelli, Sara, 25

Tran, Ying-Ying, 5
Tsai, Chen-Tse, 61
Tsai, Richard Tzong-Han, 13, 17
Tsakalidis, Adam, 21
Tseng, Chien-Hui, 57
Tu, Zhaopeng, 33

Van Durme, Benjamin, 5

Wang, Bo, 21
Wang, Boli, 29
Wang, Jui-Yang, 17
Wang, Longyue, 33
Wang, Yu-Chun, 13
Way, Andy, 33
Wolfe, Travis, 5
Wong, Ka Ming, 13
Wu, Chi-En, 53
Wu, Chun-Kai, 13
Wu, Yu-Hsuan, 49

Xu, Jiarui, 61
Xuan Khoai, Pham, 37

Zhang, Ted, 5
Zubiaga, Arkaitz, 21

Association for Computational Linguistics
209 N. Eighth Street
Stroudsburg, Pennsylvania 18360

ISBN 978-1-5108-5294-5